# PENN STATE

# DAILY
# DEVOTIONS
# FOR
# DIE-HARD
# FANS

# NITTANY LIONS

# Daily Devotions for Die-Hard Fans

## ACC
*Clemson Tigers*
*Duke Blue Devils*
*FSU Seminoles*
*Georgia Tech Yellow Jackets*
*North Carolina Tar Heels*
*NC State Wolfpack*
*Virginia Cavaliers*
*Virginia Tech Hokies*

## BIG 10
*Michigan Wolverines*
*Ohio State Buckeyes*
*Penn State Nittany Lions*

## BIG 12
*Baylor Bears*
*Oklahoma Sooners*
*Oklahoma State Cowboys*
*TCU Horned Frogs*
*Texas Longhorns*
*Texas Tech Red Raiders*

## SEC
*Alabama Crimson Tide*
*Arkansas Razorbacks*
*Auburn Tigers*
*More Auburn Tigers*
*Florida Gators*
*Georgia Bulldogs*
*More Georgia Bulldogs*
*Kentucky Wildcats*
*LSU Tigers*
*Mississippi State Bulldogs*
*Missouri Tigers*
*Ole Miss Rebels*
*South Carolina Gamecocks*
*More South Carolina Gamecocks*
*Texas A&M Aggies*
*Tennessee Volunteers*

*NASCAR*

# PENN STATE

# DAILY DEVOTIONS FOR DIE-HARD FANS

# NITTANY LIONS

# IN THE BEGINNING

**Read Genesis 1, 2:1-3.**

*"God saw all that he had made, and it was very good" (v. 1:31).*

P enn State football officially began in 1887. Or did it?

School records reflect that Penn State's first season of organized football was 1887. Those records concede, however, that a game of some sort was played between Penn State and Bucknell in November 1881. (Penn State won 9-0.) However, declares the Penn State football media guide, "the nature of the game was considered to be a rugby-style scrimmage," and "thus it is not counted as an intercollegiate football game."

For sure, Penn State fielded a team in 1887. Among the school's 170 students was George Linsz, who had played this new sport of football in Philadelphia before he enrolled at Penn State in 1887 as a freshman, bringing his football with him. Linsz paired with fellow student and enthusiast Charles C. Hildebrand to get football started on campus. They decided that "two literary societies were not enough extra-curricular activity" for the students.

James C. Mock, one of the members of the first team, recalled that the faculty had no opposition to the idea and their "first move was to organize the Penn State Athletic Association." Out of this came two games with Bucknell. That first squad had no official coach, but English Professor Nelson E. Cleaver, who had played the game, volunteered. He helped the older boys pick the

# NITTANY LIONS

best players for the team. They could have only twelve players because only twelve uniforms were available. Not surprisingly, Linsz was chosen the team captain since he had the only ball.

Penn State football began on Nov. 5, 1887, when the "Nittanymen" whipped the Bucknell boys 54-0. The losers promptly asked for a rematch, which Penn State also won 24-0 two weeks later. A later game against Dickinson College was cancelled.

History thus records that Penn State's first-ever football season was — appropriately enough — an undefeated one.

Beginnings are important, but what we make of them is even more important. Consider, for example, how far the Penn State football program has come since that first season.

Every morning, you get a gift from God: a new beginning. God hands to you as an expression of divine love a new day full of promise and the chance to right the wrongs in your life. You can use the day to pay a debt, start a new relationship, replace a burned-out light bulb, tell your family you love them, chase a dream, solve a nagging problem . . . or not.

God simply provides the gift. How you use it is up to you. People often talk wistfully about starting over or making a new beginning. God gives you the chance with the dawning of every new day.

You have the chance today to make things right — and that includes your relationship with God.

*We can use some football here.*
*— George Linsz and Charles C. Hildebrand*

**Every day is not just a dawn; it is a precious
chance to start over or begin anew.**

# LIVE ACTION

**Read James 2:14-26.**

*"Faith by itself, if it is not accompanied by action, is dead"*
*(v. 17).*

People across the country just learned what folks in South Florida already know. Occasionally, Hurricanes are just a lot of wind." So declared *Sports Illustrated's* Rick Reilly about the trash-talking Miami type of hurricane after the Nittany Lions defeated them 14-10 for the 1986 national championship.

"We played for the national championship on Sept. 27 [against Oklahoma]," bragged a Miami tackle before the Fiesta Bowl of Jan. 2, 1987. Such talk was typical of the way the Canes showed their disdain for Penn State in the days leading up to the national championship game. One Miami flanker bragged about how he would run right past State's two-time All-American linebacker Shane Conlan. "I think they're nothing," another player said of quarterback John Shaffer and running back D.J. Dozier.

The trash talk continued right through warmups. One receiver laughed in safety Ray Isom's face. Another told State cornerback Duffy Cobbs, "You shouldn't have come, you know. It's too late to turn back. You've chosen your own death row."

When it came time to actually play the game and do more than talk, however, Miami got whipped. In fact, after the game, about the only talking the receivers did was to make excuses. "The weather was cool. The ball was slippery," said one.

# NITTANY LIONS

The Hurricanes did manage a 10-7 lead with 12 minutes left in the game. On the next Canes' possession, nobody ran past Conlan as he nabbed an interception (his second of the night) and rumbled 38 yards to the Miami 5. Dozier scored from there.

The Canes tried to save themselves, moving to second and goal on the Penn State 5 with 48 seconds to play. But tackle Tim Johnson got a sack, a pass fell incomplete, and linebacker Pete Giftopoulos intercepted a last-gasp heave into the end zone.

The only thing left to say was "Penn State: National Champs."

Talk is cheap. Consider your neighbor or coworker who talks without saying anything, who makes promises she doesn't keep, who brags about his own exploits, who can always tell you how to do something but never shows up for the work.

How often have you fidgeted through a meeting, impatient to get on with the work everybody is talking about doing? You know — just as the Nittany Lions knew against Miami — that speech without action just doesn't cut it.

That principle applies in the life of a person of faith too. Merely declaring our faith isn't enough, however sincere we may be. It is putting our faith into action that shouts to the world of the depth of our commitment to Christ. Jesus' ministry was a virtual whirlwind of activity; only death stopped him. So are we charged with changing the world by always doing in the name of Jesus.

Jesus Christ is alive; so should our faith in Him be.

*They kept talking about how little our defensive backs were, but they'd never been hit by them.*
*— Shane Conlan*

**Faith that does not reveal itself in action is dead.**

# DYNASTY

**Read 2 Samuel 7:8-17.**

*"Your house and your kingdom will endure forever before me; your throne will be established forever" (v. 16).*

Before the 1990 season, the NCAA instituted a radical change in the way the collegiate fencing championship was determined. The pin-striped suits unknowingly thereby laid the groundwork for a Penn State dynasty.

Prior to 1990, Penn State was competitive in collegiate fencing, but that was all. The Lion swordsmen had never won a national championship; they had finished second in 1984 and 1989. The women fencers won a national title in 1983, the second season of distaff competition, and were runners-up in 1984.

Through the 2014 season, though, Penn State has won thirteen of the 25 national titles since 1990 and finished second eight other times. The latest crown came in 2014. At one point, the Lions ripped off six straight national championships (1995-2000). Notre Dame is the closest challenger with four titles.

So what happened that gave rise to a dynasty, other than talent, hard work, and coaching from master fencer Emmanuil Kaidanov, who was present at the first title and the 2014 one? Prior to 1990, fencers competed as individuals, and the women had a separate competition. Since 1990, though, three-member teams compete in each event and the men's and women's scores are combined. The changes have forever favored Penn State's depth.

That first team championship was a true thriller, "a scene straight out of High Noon." After four days and 88 matches, it all came down to a showdown between Penn State's Geoffrey Russell and a Columbia fencer. The event was the epee, considered "the most dramatic and least forgiving of the sport's three events." The whole body is the target; first fencer to five touches won the title. Russell, a sophomore from California, touched first — five consecutive times. A dynasty was born on that day.

Inevitably, someone will challenge the Penn State dynasty in fencing. History teaches us that kingdoms, empires, countries, and even sports programs rise and fall. Dynasties end as events and circumstances conspire and align to snap all winning streaks.

Your life is like that; you win some and lose some. You get a promotion on Monday and your son gets arrested on Friday. You breeze through your annual physical but your dog dies. You finally line up a date with that cutie next door and get sent out of town on business.

Only one dynasty will never end because it is based upon an everlasting promise from God. God promised David the king an enduring line in the appearance of one who would establish God's kingdom forever. That one is Jesus Christ, the reigning king of God's eternal and unending dynasty. The only way to lose out on that one is to stand on the sidelines and not get in the game.

*Dynasties, streaks, and careers all come to an end eventually.*
— ESPN's Mr. Clean

**All dynasties and win streaks end except the one**
**God established with Jesus as its king;**
**this one never loses and never will.**

# IN THE KNOW

**Read John 4:19-26, 39-42.**

*"They said to the woman, . . . 'Now we have heard for ourselves, and we know that this man really is the Savior of the world'" (v. 42).*

**K**erry Collins just knew. As a result, the Nittany Lions got a thrilling win over Michigan that propelled them toward the Big Ten championship, the Rose Bowl, and an undefeated season.

The 1994 Lions ripped through the storied Big Ten in only their second year of competition in the new league. They were the first team in the history of the Big Ten to post a 12-0 record and went on to whip Oregon 38-20 in Pasadena. Five offensive players were first-team All-America: quarterback Collins, tight end Kyle Brady, tailback Ki-Jana Carter, wide receiver Bobby Engram, and guard Jeff Hartings.

On Oct. 15, the team traveled to Ann Arbor for what was called "the Big Ten confrontation of the year." Penn State was 5-0 and ranked No. 2 in the country. Michigan had only a one-point loss to Colorado to mar its season.

As expected, they battled all afternoon. Penn State jumped out to a 16-3 lead before the Wolverines roared back to lead 17-16. The score was knotted at 24 in the fourth quarter when Collins led the high-flying offense down the field. With only three minutes left to play, they faced third and 11 at the Michigan 16. Once he was under center, Collins looked over the Wolverine defense.

# NITTANY LIONS

When his back went in motion, the Nittany Lion quarterback just knew his team was about to score.

Collins saw a Michigan safety follow the Penn State back. That left Engram with one-on-one coverage; the Michigan defensive back had no help coming over the middle. "As soon as I saw that safety move up," Collins said, "my eyes just lit up. I knew exactly where I was going with the ball."

Engram crossed smoothly over the middle and squared himself toward his quarterback. Collins threw a strike for the game-winning touchdown. Just as he had known would happen.

Kerry Collins just knew Penn State would score in the same way you know certain things in your life. That your spouse loves you, for instance. That you are good at your job. That a bad day fishing is still better than a good day at work. That with all its problems the USA is still the greatest country in the world. You know these things even though no mathematician or philosopher can prove any of this on paper.

It's the same way with faith in Jesus: You just know that he is God's son and the savior of the world. You know it in the same way that you know Penn State is the only team worth pulling for: with every fiber of your being, with all your heart, your mind, and your soul.

You just know, and because you know him, Jesus knows you. And that is all you really need to know.

*Players don't care how much I know until they know how much I care.*
*— Former college football coach Frosty Westering*

**A life of faith is lived in certainty and conviction:**
**You just know you know.**

# COMEBACK KIDS

**Read Acts 9:1-22.**

*"All those who heard him were astonished and asked,
'Isn't he the man who raised havoc in Jerusalem among
those who call on this name?'" (v. 21)*

They had a brutal first quarter. They had to come back not once but twice. But the 2005 Nittany Lions did it to beat Northwestern.

On Sept. 24, Penn State opened the Big Ten portion of what would be a sensational 11-1 season. Little was sensational, though, about State's play early on. When the first quarter finally ended, Northwestern led 10-0 and had rolled up 155 yards to State's 11. Four seconds into the second quarter, the lead stretched to 13-0.

The Lions appeared to have finally gotten themselves together when freshman Justin King caught a 37-yard touchdown pass from senior quarterback Michael Robinson to cap an 80-yard drive. Northwestern promptly ripped off ten straight points to open up a 23-7 lead. But the Wildcats were never able to put the Lions completely away. They left room for a comeback.

Robinson got the rally started with a 26-yard strike to wide receiver Deon Butler, a redshirt freshman who would lead the team for the season with 37 catches and nine touchdowns. That left the Lions still alive as they regrouped at halftime trailing 23-14. "In the second half, we just lined up and played football," said linebacker Paul Posluszny. "That seemed to work really well for us."

Indeed. Two field goals from Kevin Kelly cut the lead to 23-20, and Penn State finally completed the comeback when Robinson scored from eight yards out with less than nine minutes to play. But the 27-26 lead didn't hold up as Northwestern pulled a comeback of its own to lead 29-27.

One more rally. Robinson led the Comeback Kids on an 80-yard drive in one minute, 19 seconds. He hit freshman Derrick Williams for a 36-yard touchdown with 51 seconds left for the 34-29 comeback win.

Life will have its setbacks whether they result from personal failures or from forces and people beyond your control. Being a Christian and a faithful follower of Jesus Christ doesn't insulate you from getting into deep trouble

Maybe financial problems suffocated you. A serious illness put you on the sidelines. Or your family was hit with a great tragedy. Life is a series of victories and defeats. That means winning isn't about avoiding defeat; it's about getting back up to compete again. It's about making a comeback of your own.

When you avail yourself of God's grace and God's power, your comeback is always greater than your setback. You are never too far behind, and it's never too late in life's game for Jesus to lead you to victory, to turn trouble into triumph. As it was with the Nittany Lions against Northwestern and with the apostle Paul, it's not how you start that counts; it's how you finish.

*We needed this kind of [comeback] win to boost our team.*
*— Wide receiver Isaac Smolko*

**In life, victory is truly a matter of how you finish
and whether you finish with Jesus at your side.**

# GOOD LUCK

**Read 1 Samuel 28:3-20.**

*"Saul then said to his attendants, 'Find me a woman who is a medium, so I may go and inquire of her'" (v. 7).*

One of the school's all-time leading scorers. A three time All-Big Ten point guard. A six-time national coach of the year. They were all factors in the Lady Lions' great 28-3 season of 1993-94. Surely, though, the pennies had something to do with it all.

In only their second season in the league, the Lady Lions tied for first in the Big Ten with a 16-2 league record in 1993-94. Coach Rene Portland's squad was led by sophomore Tina Nicholson, the rather diminutive (5'3") star point guard, and junior guard Katina Mack, who would be drafted by the pros.

Nicholson started her athletic career playing football against the boys. When she was in the third grade, she pestered her father until he let her play midget football. She towered over the boys and had to lose weight to reach the league limit. "It was the only time I've ever been too big," said Nicholson, who was the league's star. She scored 21 touchdowns and outscored a player named Clint Seace, who went on to play football for Penn State.

The 1993-94 team started the season 18-0, which became quite painful for Portland as she attempted to follow a tradition that had begun with the 1990-91 season. Her youngest child, Stephen, who was 8, presented her with a lucky penny; she tucked it into her left shoe. After every win, he gave her another penny to put into her shoe. They kept winning, starting 11-0. After the first loss, Stephen told his mom to throw the pennies away "because they don't work anymore."

In 1993-94, Portland was at the Wisconsin game with sixteen pennies inside the arch of a high-heeled shoe. "They hurt," she confessed. But she wouldn't break the superstition as long as the Lady Lions were winning.

Black cats are right pretty. A medium is a steak. And what in the world is a blarney stone? About as superstitious as you get is to say "God bless you" when somebody sneezes.

You look indulgently upon good-luck charms like lucky pennies, tarot cards, astrology, palm readers, and the like; they're really just amusing and harmless. So what's the problem? Nothing as long as you conduct yourself with the belief that superstitious objects and rituals — whether it's broken mirrors or your daily horoscope — can't bring about good or bad luck. You just aren't willing to let such foolish notions and nonsense have a place of any importance or influence your life.

The danger of superstition lies in its ability to lure you into trusting it, thus allowing it some degree of influence over your life. In that case, it subverts God's rightful place.

Whether or not it's superstition, something does rule your life. It should be God — and God alone.

*Sure, luck means a lot in football. Not having a good quarterback is bad luck.*
*— Legendary NFL coach Don Shula*

**Superstitions may not rule your life, but something does; it should be God and God alone.**

# NAME DROPPING

**Read Exodus 3:13-20.**

*"God said to Moses, 'I AM WHO I AM. This is what you are to say to the Israelites: 'I AM has sent me to you''" (v. 14).*

Penn State's first All-American football player had a nickname that seems strange for one of the toughest players in school history, but it actually fit his life quite well.

William T. Dunn played center and linebacker and was captain of the 1906 squad that shut out nine opponents and allowed only ten points all season. That season he became the first player outside of the Ivy League to be named All-America, the first great linebacker from "Linebacker U."

A writer described Dunn as "a powerful charger on offense" and "a terror to opponents on defense." He was also one tough hombre. He once played against Navy with a broken collarbone and tossed aside crutches to play his last game against Pitt.

And his nickname? Mother. William T. "Mother" Dunn. In his official capacity as president of the freshman class, he was leading his classmates across campus one day when a sophomore student shouted out, "There goes Mother Dunn and all her baby chicks." The nickname stuck.

After his college days, Dunn went to medical school and did indeed become something of a "Mother" to a whole flock. He went into virtual seclusion as the plantation doctor on what was then the isolated island of Maui. He took such great care of the island folk that he once lost a finger after he refused to wear protective gloves while he was working with a patient under X-ray equipment. He felt the glove hindered his work.

Even in the case of William T. Dunn and his rather interesting moniker, nicknames are usually not slapped haphazardly upon individuals but rather reflect widely held perceptions about the person named. Proper names do that also; we hear the name of someone we know, and images and perceptions arise unbidden.

Nowhere throughout history has this concept been more prevalent than in the Bible, where a name is not a mere label but is an expression of the essential nature of the named one. That is, a person's name reveals his or her character. Even God shares this concept; to know the name of God is to know God as he has chosen to reveal himself to us.

What does your name say about you? Honest, trustworthy, a seeker of the truth and a person of God? Or does the mention of your name cause your coworkers to whisper snide remarks, your neighbors to roll their eyes, or your friends to start making allowances for you?

Most importantly, what does your name say about you to God? He, too, knows you by name.

*A good nickname inspires awe and ensures that you'll be enshrined in the Pantheon of [Sports] Legends.*

— *Funny Sports Quotes blog*

**Live so that your name evokes
positive associations by people you know,
by the public, and by God.**

# WHO, ME?

**Read Judges 6:11-23.**

*"'But Lord,' Gideon asked, 'how can I save Israel? My clan is the weakest in Manasseh, and I am the least in my family'" (v. 15).*

**W**ho, me?" Not surprisingly, that was pretty much Joe Nastasi's reaction when a coach told him he was going to win the Michigan game on Saturday.

The Nittany Lions of 1995 were 6-3 and ranked 19th when they hosted the 13th-ranked Wolverines on Nov. 18 in what became known as the Snow Bowl. Nineteen inches of snow blanketed State College the week of the game. Hundreds of volunteers, including students and low-security prison inmates, were called in to clear the field, the seats, and the walkways. A few snowballs pelted the players but otherwise the game went on.

Nastasi, a redshirt freshman wide receiver, was among those to get smacked. "Those things were stinging," he recalled. Nastasi went into that game with a heightened sense of anticipation. He was the holder for Brett Conway on field goals and extra points. Earlier in the week, offensive coordinator Franny Ganter surprised Nastasi by telling him, "Joe, you're gonna be the hero this week."

Nastasi's first reaction was "What are you talking about?" "We have a little something, a little wrinkle we're throwing in," Ganter said. So they watched film together with the coach pointing out how Michigan overloaded their right side on field goals, making them vulnerable to a fake. "We just pulled a guard and kicked the guy out," Nastasi recalled. "It was pretty easy."

Throughout the game, Nastasi waited for the chance to make the call for the fake. The chance came with 2:40 left and the Lions leading 20-17. "It was perfect," Nastasi remembered. "I just took the snap, picked it up and ran." He got a crushing block from guard Jeff Hartings and scored to clinch the 27-17 win.

Like Joe Nastasi, you've experienced that moment of surprise with its "who, me?" feeling. Sometimes it's downright unpleasant. How about that time the teacher called on you when you hadn't done a lick of homework? Or the night the hypnotist pulled you out of a room full of folks to be his guinea pig? You've had the wide-eyed look and the turmoil in your midsection when you were suddenly singled out and found yourself in a situation you neither sought nor were prepared for.

You may feel the same way Gideon did about being called to serve God in some way, quailing at the very notion of being audacious enough to teach Sunday school, lead a small group study, or coordinate a high school prayer club. After all, who's worthy enough to do anything like that?

The truth is that nobody is — but that doesn't seem to matter to God. And it's his opinion, not yours, that counts.

*I thought we were going to win right up until they converted the fake field goal.*

*— Michigan head coach Lloyd Carr*

**You're right in that no one is worthy to serve God, but the problem is that doesn't matter to God.**

# DOWN AND DIRTY

**Read Isaiah 1:15-20.**

*"Though your sins are like scarlet, they shall be as white as snow; though they are red as crimson, they shall be like wool" (v. 18).*

**N**icole Fawcett owned up to it: She was a dirty girl.

An outside hitter, Fawcett completed her career at Penn State in 2008 as one of college volleyball's game's greatest players ever. She was the 2008 National Player of the Year, joining Lauren Cacciamani as Nittany Lions to win the honor. (Megan Hodge would earn the honor in 2009. See Devotion No. 88.) She was a four-time All-America and three times was All-Big Ten. She was the league's Player of the Year in 2008.

Thus, it was fitting that a front-page newspaper photo showed Fawcett hoisting the trophy when the 2008 team returned to State College after winning their second straight national title by beating Stanford in the finals. The party was a birthday gathering for Fawcett in a way; she turned 21.

So why would Fawcett confess to being "the dirty girl"? Well, under her winter coat and sweats as she raised the trophy — almost 24 hours after the Stanford match had begun in California — Fawcett still had on her uniform. She had yet to take a shower. "I didn't smell, I don't think," Fawcett said. "If I did, I didn't care because it was my birthday."

After celebrating on the court and then enduring the requisite post-game interviews, Fawcett and the gang partied together before heading home. On the long flight, Fawcett realized her uniform was still inside her sweats. "We came back and immediately started celebrating," she said. "I didn't want to leave everyone. It didn't dawn on me to get in the shower and change." Fellow senior Melissa Walbridge had an explanation for her teammate's lack of hygiene. "That's what a national championship does to you," she said. "You don't even think about things like that."

Like Nicole Fawcett, you've probably missed a shower or two. You've worked on your car, planted a garden, traipsed around in the rain, or endured some military training. You've been dirty.

Dirt, grime, and mud aren't the only sources of stains, however. We can also get dirty spiritually by not living in accordance with God's commands, by doing what's wrong, or by not doing what's right. We all experience temporary shortcomings and failures; we all slip and fall into the mud.

Whether we stay there or not, though, is a function of our relationship with Jesus. For the followers of Jesus, sin is not a way of life; it's an abnormality, so we don't stay in the filth. We seek a spiritual bath by expressing regret and asking for God's pardon in Jesus' name. God responds by washing our soul white as snow with his forgiveness.

*I was pretty disgusting when we got back to State College. I don't think I've ever felt so gross in my entire life.*
*— Nicole Fawcett on her lack of shower time*

**When your soul gets dirty, a powerful and thorough cleansing agent is available for the asking: God's forgiveness.**

# THE PRIZE

**Read Philippians 3:10-16.**

*"I press on toward the goal to win the prize for which God has called me heavenward in Christ Jesus" (v. 14).*

John Cappelletti's Heisman-Trophy acceptance speech started out with the usual forgettable thank-you's. What followed, however, was the most memorable Heisman speech in history, one that eventually would touch untold millions of lives.

Joe Paterno once declared Cappelletti to be "the best football player I ever coached." As a senior running back, he led the Lions to a 12-0 season in 1973 by rushing for 1,522 yards and scoring 17 touchdowns.

In a New York ballroom in December, Cappelletti accepted his Heisman. He thanked his teammates, his coaches, and his mother and his father. And then he spoke of Joey and his tears began. John's younger brother was 11 at the time. When he was 5, he had been diagnosed with leukemia.

"They say I've shown courage on the football field," John said. "But for me, it's only on the field and only in the fall. Joey lives with pain all the time. His courage is round the clock. I want him to have this trophy. It's more his than mine, because he's been such an inspiration to me." Amidst thunderous applause and sobs, John Cappelletti went straight to the family table to hug Joey.

Before the '73 West Virginia game, Joey asked his brother to score four touchdowns for him as a birthday present. Knowing such a feat was unlikely, John nevertheless promised. He scored three times in the 62-14 romp before he headed for the bench. But teammate and friend Eddie O'Neil went to Joe Paterno and told him about Cappelletti's promise. Paterno put him back in, called his number, and Cappelletti scored his fourth touchdown. Joey died on April 8, 1976 with John at his bedside. The brothers' story was made into the movie *Something for Joey* in 1977.

Even the most modest and self-effacing among us can't help but be pleased by prizes and honors. They symbolize the approval and appreciation of others, whether it's an Employee of the Month award, a plaque for sales achievement, a Heisman Trophy, or the sign declaring yours as the neighborhood's prettiest yard.

Such prizes and awards are often the culmination of the pursuit of personal achievement and accomplishment. They represent accolades and recognition from the world. Nothing is inherently wrong with any of that as long as we keep them in perspective.

That is, we must never let awards become such idols that we worship or lower our sight from the greatest prize of all and the only one truly worth winning. It's one that won't rust, collect dust, or leave us wondering why we worked so hard to win it in the first place. It's offered freely to us; we have only to accept it.

The ultimate prize is eternal life, and it's ours through Jesus Christ.

*Johnny just gave you his Heisman Trophy.*
*— John Cappelletti, Sr. to Joey, who asked what was going on*

**The greatest prize of all doesn't require competition to claim it; God has it ready to hand to you through Jesus Christ.**

# THE PIONEER SPIRIT

**Read Luke 5:1-11.**

*"So they pulled their boats up on shore, left everything and followed him" (v. 11).*

With a few belongings, a letter to the Penn State football coach, and only a vague idea where State College was, Wally Triplett left home in 1945 to make history.

Triplett wasn't the first African-American football player to suit up for the Lions. Early in the 1940s, Dave Alston, whom coach Bob Higgins called "the greatest player I ever coached," had broken the color line. Alston was, in fact, Triplett's boyhood idol. But Alston died suddenly in 1941 after a tonsillectomy and never lettered.

Triplett's success at Penn State would blaze a trail for others to follow. He was the first African-American to start and to letter for the Nittany Lions. As a senior in 1948, he led the Lions in scoring and all-purpose yardage. In 1949, he became the first African-American draftee to play in the NFL.

Triplett's influence ultimately went far beyond State College when the 9-0 Lions of 1947 accepted an invitation to play in the Cotton Bowl in Dallas. Triplett was one of three black players on this unusually seasoned team that included veterans who had returned from World War II. During the season, the Lions were scheduled to play in Miami with the stipulation that the black players could not suit up. Triplett said, "That's when the shock of my life came." The players refused to abide by the blatantly racial restriction. White players like Neg Norton and John Potsklan told the coaches, "We play together, we stay together." Penn State didn't make the trip.

None of the hotels in Dallas would house the Lions because of the African-American players, so some alums arranged for the team to stay on a naval base eighteen miles outside of town. On Jan. 1, 1948, Wally Triplett blazed another trail when he broke the color barrier in the Cotton Bowl. State and SMU tied 13-13.

Going to a place in your life you've never been before requires a willingness to take risks and face uncertainty head-on. You may have never helped change the landscape of college football, but you've had your moments when your latent pioneer spirit manifested itself. That time you changed careers, volunteered at a homeless shelter, learned Spanish, or went back to school.

While attempting new things invariably begets apprehension, the truth is that when life becomes too comfortable and too familiar, it gets boring. The same is true of God, who is downright dangerous because he calls us to be anything but comfortable as we serve him. He summons us to continuously blaze new trails in our faith life, to follow him no matter what.

Stepping out on faith is risky all right, but the reward is a life of accomplishment, adventure, and joy that cannot be equaled anywhere else.

*This is life. Let's live it and not be afraid.*

— *Wally Triplett*

**Unsafe and downright dangerous, God calls us
out of the place where we are comfortable to a life
of adventure and trailblazing in his name.**

DAY 12

# BROKEN DREAMS

**Read Joel 2:28-32.**

*"I will pour out my Spirit on all people. . . . Your old men will dream dreams" (v. 28).*

Franco Harris' childhood dream was to follow in his father's footsteps. Penn State football fans remain grateful to this day that the dream never came true.

Harris was the third of nine children born to Cad and Gina Harris. His dad was a military man who met Gina while serving in Italy during World War II. Harris was born on and grew up close to Fort Dix, New Jersey, in a community in which other children and games were a constant. He played everything from dodgeball to basketball and softball.

But they were just kid games, nothing to be taken seriously. Harris "never wasted time dreaming about some glorious pro football career that awaited him after college." Such a notion was foreign to the family. "Coming from Italy, my mother knew nothing about sports," Harris said. His dad never played sports.

Instead, Harris' boyhood dream was to be a soldier just like his dad, maybe even an Army Ranger. But older brother Mario was offered a partial scholarship to play football at Glassboro State. "I was in shock," Franco recalled. "Everybody was in shock. Because no one had ever mentioned the word college to us in our whole life."

Now Franco gradually surrendered one dream for another. He

# NITTANY LIONS

was a high All-America in 1966, and when he accepted a full ride to Penn State, his mom was ecstatic. Franco said, "She would tell the three youngest boys, she'd say, 'Go out and kicka tha football, go, go, go. Go out and kicka tha football.' It was funny."

Harris scored 25 career touchdowns for the Lions and rushed for more than 2,000 yards. His three teams of 1969-71 were 29-4 and won two bowl games. Harris, of course, went on to become a pro football legend with the Steelers.

Who would have dreamed it?

Like Franco Harris, we all have particular dreams. Perhaps to make a million dollars, write the Great American Novel, or find the perfect spouse. More likely than not, though, we gradually lose our hold on those dreams. They slip away from us as we surrender them to the reality of everyday living.

But we also have general dreams. For world peace or for an end to hunger. That no child should ever again be afraid. These dreams we hold doggedly onto as if something inside us tells us that even though the world gets itself into a bigger mess every year, one day everything will be all right.

That's because it will be. God has promised a time when his spirit will rule the world. Jesus spoke of a time when he will return to claim his kingdom. In that day, our dreams of peace and plenty and the banishment of hate and want will be reality.

Our dreams based on God's promises will come true.

*To achieve in sports you first have to have a dream, and then you must act on that dream.*
*— Speed skater Dianne Holum*

**Dreams based on God's promises will come true.**

# CLOCKWORK

**Read Matthew 25:1-13.**

*"Keep watch, because you do not know the day or the hour" (v. 13).*

**B**ecause of a clock, Penn State eventually landed a coaching legend whose very sport depended upon the clock.

Harry Groves didn't know what he wanted to do with his life after his 1953 graduation from Temple where he was a middle distance runner on the track team. He set two years aside to find out, taking a job with the U.S. Army as quartermaster at Fort Eustis, Va. The job proved very educational; among other things it taught him he didn't want to keep it.

The young Groves found himself staring at a wall clock every afternoon at four. Daily, he thought the same thing: "This is terrible; this is what I'm going to do for the rest of my life — look at a clock to try to get out?" He eventually reached a rather odd conclusion: "I thought, 'Track is the only thing I've ever done that there was no clock involved.'" Track, of course, lives and dies by the clock — but in a way totally different from the excruciating clockwatching Groves was daily subjected to.

Groves spent one year as a graduate assistant track coach at William and Mary, and when the head coach resigned in 1956, he took over the program. He had found his calling in life. For thirteen years, he led the program to excellence and was uninterested in doing anything else until the Penn State head coaching position opened up in 1968. "I just jumped at applying," he said. The rest is Penn State legend. Groves retired in 2006 after a 38-year career at State College that saw him inducted into the coaches association's hall of fame in 2001. He was five times the national coach of the year, and his Lion teams won more than 85 percent of their dual meets. Between William & Mary and Penn State, Groves coached twenty-one national champions, fourteen Olympians, and 227 All-Americas.

And it all started with that clock on the wall.

We may pride ourselves on our time management, but the truth is that we don't manage time; it manages us. Hurried and harried, we live by schedules that seem to have too much what and too little when. By setting the bedside alarm at night, we even let the clock determine how much down time we get. A life of leisure actually means one in which time is of no importance.

Every second of our life — all the time we have — is a gift from God, who dreamed up time in the first place. We would do well, therefore, to consider what God considers to be good time management. After all, Jesus himself warned us against mismanaging the time we have.

From God's point of view, using our time wisely means being prepared at every moment for Jesus' return, which will occur — well, only time will tell when.

*We didn't lose the game; we just ran out of time.*

— *Vince Lombardi*

**We mismanage our time when we fail
to prepare for Jesus' return even though
we don't know when that will be.**

# HOMELESS

**Read Matthew 8:18-22.**

*"Jesus replied, 'Foxes have holes and birds of the air have nests, but the Son of Man has no place to lay his head'"* (v. 20).

hen you play in the second largest stadium in the country and the fourth largest in the world as Penn State does, you naturally have a lot of home games each season. Once upon a time, though, the Nittany Lions were virtually homeless in their quest to play big-time football games.

Well into the twentieth century, geography forced Penn State to leave home. As Robert Maxwell of the *Philadelphia Public Ledger* wrote, "State College is located in Center [sic] County, and Center County can be located by means of a large map, a compass, and an experienced guide. [I]t is a very hard place to get to and for that reason most of the big games are played away from home."

As a result, many of the home games weren't against major competition. For instance, Penn State's 1920 schedule included Lebanon Valley, Gettysburg, and Muhlenberg, none of which played major ball. To gain some national exposure, the schedule was seriously upgraded in 1921. As Maxwell pointed out, however, "It is impossible [for Penn State] to get good teams on the home grounds, so it is necessary to go someplace else."

The 1921 squad thus hit the road in a manner that has probably never been equaled during the regular season. The team was in the midst of a 30-game unbeaten streak and went 8-0-2. The Lions traveled — This was in 1921, remember, when getting around was a lot more difficult than it is now. — 8,500 miles. They visited Seattle, Philadelphia, New York, Pittsburgh, and Cambridge.

Along the way, these indomitable road warriors beat Georgia Tech in New York, Navy in Philadelphia, and Washington on its home field, and tied Harvard and Pitt. The traveling may have left the team feeling homeless, but it worked. The next season the Lions were in the Rose Bowl.

Rock bottom in America has a face: the bag lady pushing a shopping cart; the scruffy guy with a beard and a backpack at the interstate exit holding a cardboard sign. Look closer at that bag lady or that scruffy guy, though, and you may see desperate women with children fleeing violence, veterans haunted by their combat experiences, or sick or injured workers.

Few of us are indifferent to the homeless when we're around them. They often raise quite strong passions, whether we regard them as a ministry or a nuisance. They trouble us, perhaps because we realize that we're only one catastrophic illness and a few paychecks away from joining them. They remind us, therefore, of how tenuous our hold upon material success really is.

But they also stir our compassion because we serve a Lord who — like them — had no home, and for whom, the homeless, too, are his children.

*The Nittany Lions were starting to be called the 'Nittany Nomads.'*
*— Sports editor Robert Maxwell on Penn State's 1921 travels*

**Because they, too, are God's children,**
**the homeless merit our compassion, not our scorn.**

# DRY RUN

**Read John 4:1-15.**

*"Everyone who drinks this water will be thirsty again,
but whoever drinks the water I give him will never thirst.
Indeed, the water I give him will become in him a spring
of water welling up to eternal life" (vv. 13-14).*

The drought was over. Five straight times the Nittany Lions had walked into the Big House, and five straight times they had lost. No more.

Joe Paterno had tried hard to convince his players that the Oct. 24, 2009, game against Michigan was just another contest, but they knew otherwise. If the especially intense practices the week of the game or Paterno's fiery Friday night pep talk and his emotional pregame speech hadn't convinced them, his attitude in the tunnel waiting for Michigan to take the field would have convinced all doubters. They saw a man determined to end his team's five-game losing streak in Ann Arbor. "We looked over at Joe," said quarterback Daryll Clark, "and he's jumping up and down. I'm like, 'OK, it's time to play some football.'"

And play the Lions did. They spotted the Wolverines a sudden touchdown and then roared the rest of the afternoon. They tied the game less than two minutes after the Michigan score and were off and romping to a 35-10 stomping.

Clark completed 16 of 27 passes for 230 yards and four touchdowns, three to wide receiver Graham Zug, the fourth a 60-yard bomb to tight end Andrew Quarless. Tailback Evan Royster ran for 100 yards on 20 carries. The defense held the Big Ten's best rushing team to 110 yards on 40 tries — only 74 yards after that opening possession — and to 3-of-15 conversions on third down.

"This victory is a little bit sweeter for us," said defensive end Jerome Hayes, referring to the end of the five-game losing streak in the Big House that had stretched back to 1998.

You can walk across that river you boated on in the spring and barely get your ankles wet. The city's put all neighborhoods on water restriction, and that beautiful lawn you fertilized and seeded is well on its way toward tuning a sickly, pale green. It may lapse all the way to brown. Somebody wrote "Wash Me" on the rear window of your truck; it didn't strike you as funny.

The sun bakes everything, including the concrete. The earth itself seems exhausted, just barely hanging on. It's a drought.

It's the way a soul looks that shuts God out.

God instilled thirst in us to warn us of our body's need for physical water. He also gave us a spiritual thirst that can be quenched only by his presence in our lives. Without God, we are like spiritual tumbleweeds, dried out and windblown in our souls, offering the illusion of life where there is only death.

Living water — water of life — is readily available in Jesus. We may drink our fill, and thus we slake our thirst and end our soul's drought — forever.

*It got through to us how much this game meant not only to [Coach Joe Paterno] but to Penn State.*

— *Punter Jeremy Boone*

**Our soul thirsts for God's refreshing presence.**

# HEART OF THE MATTER

**Read 1 Samuel 13:1-14.**

*"The Lord has sought out a man after his own heart" (v. 14).*

The size of the Penn State roster indicated certain defeat. The size of the heart of those players dictated otherwise.

On Jan. 3, 2004, extraordinary circumstances combined to foreshadow certain defeat for the PSU men's basketball team against the Bucknell Bisons. Four days after the team's second-leading scorer left the squad for personal reasons, first-year Penn State coach Ed DeChellis was trying to keep his team together. "As a staff we went back to work and got on guys and said, 'Let's go,'" DeChellis said. "We can't feel sorry for ourselves."

So what was all the fuss about one player up and leaving? Why were DeChellis and his coaches so concerned about his players appearing downtrodden and frustrated?

Well, they were kind of shorthanded.

Against the Bisons, only six Nittany Lions played. That's six — including two freshmen. "You like our rotation?" DeChellis joked after the game. He could laugh despite the adversity because his six-man team came from behind, outrebounded the Bisons 33-27, and won the game 58-46. Penn State trailed for most of the first half, and then used a 16-4 run to take a 41-33 lead with 8:51 left to play. The Lions never fell behind again.

The win came despite Bucknell's superior depth. The Bisons

rotated fourteen players in and out of the game. Penn State freshmen Ben Luber, who scored 11 points, and Marion Smith, who had 15 points, played all forty minutes. "The two freshmen kids," DeChellis said. "I think they can run all night. I don't know if they'll run all night in February, but they can run all night now."

The Bucknell coach admitted he used his depth to try to tire the Lion players out. To no avail. The Nittany Lions didn't have the numbers, but they did have the heart.

We all face trying circumstances such as what the Penn State basketball team was up against in the Bucknell game. Sometimes, though we fight with all we have, we lose. Even Penn State loses games, no matter how hard the players fight.

At some time, you probably have admitted you were whipped no matter how much it hurt. Always in your life, though, you have known that you would fight for some things with all your heart and never give them up: your family, your country, your friends, your core beliefs.

God should be on that list too. God seeks men and women who will never turn their back on him because they are people after God's own heart. That is, they will never betray God with their unbelief; they will never lose their childlike trust in God; they will never cease to love God with all their heart.

They are lifetime members of God's team; it's a mighty good one to be on, but it takes heart.

*It is not the size of a man but the size of his heart that matters.*
*— Evander Holyfield*

**To be on God's team requires
the heart of a champion.**

# RECIPE FOR DISASTER

**Read Luke 21:5-11, 25-28.**

*"There will be great earthquakes, famines and pestilences in various places, and fearful events and great signs from heaven" (v. 11).*

**P**enn State's trip to Florida for the 1961 Gator Bowl was just an unmitigated disaster. Until the football game.

The Nittany Lions of Coach Rip Engle went 7-3 and received the bowl invitation to play Georgia Tech. Right away, apprehension about the trip arose in the State camp. End Dave Robinson, who would be All-America in 1962 and would be inducted into the College Football Hall of Fame in 1997, would be the first African-American to play in the Gator Bowl. One of the enduring stories of Penn State football is that he stepped off the plane in Florida wearing sunglasses. When Engle questioned him about being a hot dog, Robinson supposedly replied, "No, coach, but when I travel in the South, I travel incognito."

The uneasiness was not unwarranted. The airport restaurant refused to serve Robinson; the whole walked out. The Lions had to stay down the road in St. Augustine because no hotels in Jacksonville would rent Robinson a room.

But that was just the beginning. When the team showed up to tour the Gator Bowl, the gate was locked. When they arrived for a scheduled practice, they discovered the Tech band rehearsing on the field. The Lions worked out in a parking lot. Engle repeatedly missed television interviews. "I just get so wrapped up in other things, I don't remember to show up," he explained. Writers questioned whether Penn State belonged in the game at all.

The beginning of the contest contributed to the perception that the trip was one big disaster as Tech jumped out to a 9-0 lead. Penn State recovered, though, to win easily 30-15. Turned out, that trip wasn't so bad after all.

We live in a world constantly plagued by short-term and seemingly permanent disasters that are on a much greater scale than the troubles the Lions encountered in Jacksonville. Earthquakes virtually obliterate an entire nation; volcanoes erupt and change the climate; children starve to death every day. Floods devastate cities; oil pollutes our oceans and seashores. Can we even count the number of wars that are going on at any one time?

This apparently unending litany of disaster is enough to make us all give up hope. Maybe — but not for the followers of Jesus Christ. The truth is that Jesus' disciples should find reassurance of their ultimate hope in the world's constant disasters because this is exactly what Jesus said would happen.

These disasters indicate that the time of our redemption is drawing near. How near is up to God to decide. Nevertheless, this is a season of hope and great promise for those of the faith.

*The minute you think you've got it made, disaster is just around the corner.*

*— Joe Paterno*

**Jesus told us what to do when disaster**
**threatens to overwhelm us and our world:**
**'Stand up and lift up your heads.'**

# CONFIDENCE MAN

**Read Micah 7:5-7.**

*"As for me, I will look to the Lord, I will wait for the God of my salvation" (v. 7 NRSV).*

Eighteen-year-old Craig Fayak was really apprehensive — and then absolutely nothing happened to boost his confidence.

"Son, this is gonna be a big week in your life," a coach told the freshman on Monday, Sept. 10, 1990. Fayak didn't understand at all until he opened his locker to get ready for practice and found a blue jersey. He was the team's number one kicker.

He hadn't expected it. He had been behind two kickers on the depth chart and expected to be redshirted. In the season opener, though, the starting kicker missed two field goals, and the other kicker was converted to a punter. The job was Fayak's. "I was scared to death," he said about his first game on Sept. 15 against Southern Cal on the road.

So he got his big moment: a 39-yard attempt. And he missed it. "I'd never felt so sick in my life," Fayak said. But he got sicker. The next Saturday the Lions rolled over Rutgers, but Fayak's one try was blocked, "shuttling him into an off week with brittle confidence and an ugly O-fer in the field goal column."

But two weeks later he got another chance late in the first half of the Temple game and drilled a 45-yarder. Then he kicked another in the last half. The field goals meant nothing in the 48-10 romp, but they meant everything to Fayak and his confidence.

The following week his two field goals were the difference in a 27-21 win over Syracuse. "The roll, as it goes, was on."

And it never stopped. The confident Fayak led Penn State in scoring for three of his four seasons. In 1992, he hit a school-record thirteen straight field goals. He finished as State's all-time leading scorer and set a record with fifty field goals in his career (both marks broken by kicker Kevin Kelly 2005-08).

You need confidence in all areas of your life. You're confident the company you work for will pay you on time, or you wouldn't go to work. You turn the ignition without thinking about it, confident your car will start. When you flip a switch, you expect the light to come on.

Confidence in other people and in things is often misplaced, however. Companies go broke; car batteries die; light bulbs burn out. Even the people you love the most sometimes let you down.

So where can you place your trust with absolute confidence you won't be betrayed? In the promises of God.

Such confidence is easy when everything's going your way, but what about when you cry as Micah did, "What misery is mine!" As Micah declares, that's when your confidence in God must be its strongest. That's when you wait for the Lord confident that God will not fail you, that he will never let you down.

*Confidence for an athlete is a funny thing. You don't know how you get it or lose it. But you know when you have it.*

— Craig Fayak

**People, things, and organizations
will let you down; only God
can be trusted absolutely and confidently.**

# LESSON LEARNED

**Read Psalm 143.**

*"Teach me to do your will, for you are my God" (v. 10).*

During a game, one Nittany Lion learned a valuable lesson: The line between being brave and being dumb is a thin one.

Dick Harlow was a two-year football letterman (1910-11) at Penn State and a member of the Nittany Lion baseball and track teams. He was the first Penn State graduate to return as the head coach (1915-17), compiling a 20-8 record across his three seasons. He went on to coach at Colgate and Harvard, making more history as the first non-alumnus ever to coach at the latter school. He was inducted into the College Football Hall of Fame in 1954.

During his playing days, Harlow broke an ankle, which called for a trip to the hospital and relegation to the sideline on some crutches. But the last game of the season, the big game against Pitt, was coming up, and Harlow wanted to play.

"We made an issue of it," he recalled. "Either I played or we'd all be mad." Team captain Pete Mauthe, a four-year letterman at fullback who was inducted into the College Football Hall of Fame in 1957, argued for Harlow's right to play. In a vastly different day and age, head coach Bill Hollenback, who had three undefeated seasons in his six years as the Penn State head coach, gave in.

The trainer made a plaster cast for Harlow's leg and wrapped it around iron splints. "I came to the field on crutches," Harlow said, "and got rid of them in the field house."

Incredibly, Harlow played the full sixty minutes at his tackle position. After the game, he went back to the crutches, hobbling around on them for six weeks.

Harlow admitted he learned a lesson from the experience. "It wasn't bravery — it was dumbness," he said. "I learned that a player half as good is twice as good as a player out there with a broken leg."

Learning about anything in life requires a combination of education and experience. Education is the accumulation of facts that we call knowledge; experience is the acquisition of wisdom and discernment, which add purpose and understanding to our knowledge. Education without experience just doesn't have much practical value in our world today.

The most difficult way to learn is trial and error: dive in blindly and mess up. The best way to learn is through example coupled with a set of instructions: Someone has gone ahead to show you the way and has written down all the information you need to follow.

In teaching us the way to live godly lives, God chose the latter method. He set down in his book the habits, actions, and attitudes that make for a way of life in accordance with his wishes. He also sent us Jesus to explain and to illustrate.

God teaches us not only how to exist but how to live. We just need to be attentive students.

*If lessons are learned in defeat, our team is getting a great education.*
*— Legendary college football coach Murray Warmath*

**To learn from Jesus is to learn what life is all about and how God means for us to live it.**

### DAY 20

# IN THE BAD TIMES

### Read Philippians 1:3-14.

*"What has happened to me has really served to advance the gospel. . . . Because of my chains, most of the brothers in the Lord have been encouraged to speak the word of God more courageously and fearlessly" (vv. 12, 14).*

**P**oison ivy or a spider bite? Instead, it was leukemia.

Freshman Kari Lucas started 28 games for the Penn State softball team in 2004. In the summer, she noticed a rash on her right ankle and tossed it off as poison ivy. Later, she spotted what she thought were bug bites, perhaps a spider. When lymph nodes in her neck swelled, she underwent some tests. The diagnosis was devastating; Lucas had leukemia. "When I first heard about the disease, I cried," Lucas said. "It felt like all of the blood in my body had been drained out. I went completely numb."

But Lucas had support from her faith and her family. Inspired by her family, her faith actually grew during the worst time of her young life. Throughout her chemotherapy, she never felt like a cancer patient: "I just treated it like another conditioning workout I had to get through or another sprint I had to complete."

From the first, Lucas resolved to make it back in time for the 2005 softball season. At one point during her month-long stay in the hospital for treatment, she began to feel better and decided she needed some exercise to help her get in shape for the upcoming season. So she ran up and down the hospital stairs for an hour.

# NITTANY LIONS

When she told the doctor what she had been up to, "He was really mad and explained to me that my blood count was so low that I could have had [a heart attack]."

Kari Lucas did make it back for the 2005 season, appearing in 41 games. That fall she was pronounced to be in remission; she later declared she was "as healthy as I've ever been." She finished up at Penn State in 2007 and went on to a career as a personal fitness trainer and a high school softball coach.

Loved ones die. You're downsized. Your biopsy shows you have leukemia. Hard, tragic times are as much a part of life as noise, car repairs, and holidays are.

This applies to Christians too. Christianity is not the equivalent of a Get-out-of-Jail-Free card, granting us a lifelong exemption from either the least or the worst pain the world has to offer. While Jesus promises us he will be there to lead us through the valleys, he never promises that we will not enter them.

The question thus becomes how you handle the bad times. You can buckle to your knees in despair and cry, "Why me?" Or you can hit your knees in prayer and ask, "What do I do with this?"

Setbacks and tragedies are opportunities to reveal and to develop true character and abiding faith. Your faithfulness — not your skipping merrily along through life without pain — is what reveals the depth of your love for God.

*I don't look at my situation as, 'Why me?' I look at it as, 'OK, I have something to beat and I can help people.'*
*— Kari Lucas*

**Faithfulness to God requires faith even in —
especially in — the bad times.**

## DAY 21

# DEAD WRONG

**Read Matthew 26:14-16; 27:1-10.**

*"When Judas, who had betrayed him, saw that Jesus was condemned, he was seized with remorse" (v. 27:3).*

The Nittany Lions believed they had no shot at the national championship, and so they acted on that belief. They were wrong, however, and what they did actually cost them a shot at the title.

In the days when bowl match-ups were locked in before the regular season ended, the Nittany Lions held a team meeting on Nov. 16. 1969, to decide where they would go. They had clobbered Maryland 48-0 the day before to up their record to 7-0 on their way to an undefeated season. At the time, they were ranked third in the nation behind Ohio State and Texas.

Always wanting to play the highest-ranked team available, Joe Paterno wanted his team to go to the Cotton Bowl to play the winner of the Texas-Arkansas game. (See Devotion No. 52.) He wound up with what guard Charlie Zapiec called an "open revolt" on his hands that developed into what All-American tackle Mike Reid classified as "a disappointing set of circumstances."

Several of the African-American players did not want to go to Dallas to play, though they said they would go if the team voted to play there. Some players also said they preferred not to go to a bowl game at all if it meant being on the road at Christmas for a third straight year.

The team's vote eventually turned on its belief that it couldn't

# NITTANY LIONS

win the national championship by playing in the Cotton Bowl. The players thus voted to play Missouri in the Orange Bowl. Paterno agreed to let the team be home for Christmas.

As it turned out, however, they were wrong. When Michigan upset Ohio State, Texas moved up to No. 1. The Lions were widely perceived as having avoided the best available team, though such was not the case. They had mistakenly cost themselves a shot at the national championship.

There's wrong, there's dead wrong, and there's Judas wrong. We've all been wrong in our lives, but we can at least honestly ease our conscience by telling ourselves we'll never be as wrong as Judas was. A close examination of Judas' actions, however, reveals that we can indeed replicate in our own lives the mistake Judas made that drove him to suicidal despair.

Judas ultimately regretted his betrayal of our Lord, but his sorrow and remorse, however boundless, could not save him. His attempt to undo his initial wrong was futile because he tried to fix everything himself rather than turning to God in repentance and begging for mercy.

While we can't literally betray Jesus to his enemies as Judas did, we can match Judas' failure in our own lives by not turning to God in Jesus' name and asking for forgiveness for our sins. In that case, we ultimately will be as dead wrong as Judas was.

*When Ohio State lost, we realized we had blown a chance at the national championship.*
*— Guard Charlie Zapiec*

**A sin is the first wrong; failing to ask God**
**for forgiveness of it is the second.**

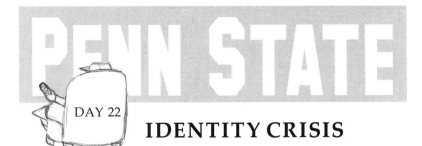

# IDENTITY CRISIS

**Read Matthew 16:13-20.**

*"[Jesus] asked his disciples, 'Who do people say the Son of Man is?' They replied, 'Some say John the Baptist; others say Elijah; and still others, Jeremiah or one of the prophets'" (vv. 13-14).*

**B**efore he was Penn State's head football coach, Bob Higgins once played in a game disguised as another, more famous player.

A two-time All-American end at Penn State, Higgins coached the Lions from 1930-1948 with an overall record of 123-83-16. His 1947 team went undefeated and tied SMU in the Cotton Bowl, Penn State's second bowl trip ever. He ended his career with ten straight winning seasons and was inducted into the College Football Hall of Fame in 1954.

Higgins was a stickler for proper decorum and dress for his players. He once chewed out a student manager because a player reported for practice wearing a huge pair of shoes that just had to be oversized. "Get this boy a pair of shoes that fit him," Higgins ordered. "Get rid of these gunboats." Then the player piped up. "Thanks coach," he said, "but these 'gunboats' fit fine. I wear size 14."

In 1920 and '21, Higgins played professional football with the Canton Bulldogs of the American Professional Football Association, the forerunner of the NFL. The legendary Jim Thorpe was a teammate, and he failed to show for a game. Team management didn't want to disappoint the crowd, so they hatched the idea of having Higgins impersonate Thorpe. His teammates taped him up to fill out Thorpe's big uniform to the point that Higgins "probably felt more like an Egyptian mummy than a football player" when he took the field.

It didn't work. When Higgins went back to field a punt, a fan yelled out, "Who's that bum in Thorpe's uniform?"

Who are you? You may not be Spider Man or the old Caped Crusader himself, but you do have a secret identity, don't you? It's hidden by the face you put on to meet the world each day, the expression that masks your secret longing to sail around the world or write a novel. Maybe you hide how much you hate your job or how badly you wish your spouse would lose weight.

You are, in fact, more than what you appear. The world does not know your depth, but you shouldn't feel too badly about the shortsightedness of others. Many people still can't figure out who Jesus is.

But that's not because Jesus failed to declare who he was; he told folks repeatedly but they failed to understand. In like manner, what matters is not what others do not know about you but what they know for sure: That you are a Christian. That, above all else, should be your identity.

*Deep inside, we're still the boys of autumn, that magic time of the year that once swept us on to America's fields.*
*— Archie Manning*

**Many folks still don't know Jesus for who he is, but everyone should recognize you as one of his followers.**

# A LONG SHOT

### Read Matthew 9:9-13.

*"[Jesus] saw a man named Matthew sitting at the tax collector's booth. 'Follow me,' he told him, and Matthew got up and followed him" (v. 9).*

That a walk-on will make the Penn State football team is a long shot. That he will see much playing time and contribute to the team is an even longer shot. That he would become the greatest receiver in school history — well, consider the odds of that. But that's exactly what Deon Butler did.

Butler was convinced that he could play major college football after high school, but few others appreciated his potential. When the big boys showed little interest in offering him a scholarship, he walked on at Penn State. Early on, the Lion coaches had him targeted as a defensive back.

What separated him from others trying to make the squad was how hard he practiced every single day. "I didn't have the luxury of having a scholarship," Butler said. "I felt like I had to go and earn it." He earned it by being the guy other players hate: the one who went as hard as he could all the time at practice. "Every day I was always practicing hard," Butler recalled.

This long shot completed his career as a Nittany Lion after the 2008 season as the school's all-time receptions leader with 179 catches. He is second all-time in total yards with 2,771 and third with 22 touchdown catches. He set the school record for receiving yards in a game with 216 yards against Northwestern in 2006.

When Butler broke a tie with Bobby Engram for career receptions with his first catch in the 34-7 defeat of Indiana on Nov. 15, 2008, no one called a time out to mark the occasion. "I'm glad we kept moving from there," Butler said. After the game, though, everyone was talking about the long shot who went from walk-on to the record books.

Matthew the tax collector was another long shot, an unlikely person to be a confidant of the Son of God. While we may not get all warm and fuzzy about the IRS, our government's revenue agents are nothing like Matthew and his ilk. He bought a franchise, paying the Roman Empire for the privilege of extorting, bullying, and stealing everything he could from his own people. The tax collectors of Jesus' time were generally considered to be "despicable, vile, unprincipled scoundrels."

And yet, Jesus said only two words to this lowlife: "Follow me." Jesus knew that this long shot would make an excellent disciple.

It's the same with us. While we may not be quite as vile as Matthew was, none of us can stand before God with our hands clean and our hearts pure. We are all impossibly long shots to enter God's Heaven. That is, until we do what Matthew did: get up and follow Jesus.

*When a kid like [Deon Butler] comes in here as a walk-on and he turns out to be as good as he is, it's great.*

— Joe Paterno

**Only through Jesus does our status change
from being long shots to enter God's Kingdom
to being heavy favorites.**

DAY 24

# RUN FOR IT

### Read John 20:1-10.

*"Peter and the other disciple started for the tomb. Both were running, but the other disciple outran Peter and reached the tomb first" (vv. 3-4).*

Annie Zinkavich had a very definite reason why she wanted nothing to do with the field hockey team: They ran too much.

When she was a freshman in high school, Zinkavich decided she wanted to be on the tennis team. And why was that? "They didn't run; they took brisk walks."

Her high school field hockey coach had other ideas, though. She came over to Zinkavich one day and issued some fateful words that would determine the course of the youngster's life: "You're going to be the goalie" on the field hockey team. Zinkavich, of course, took the news calmly and resolutely, right? Uh, not at all. "I cried for a week and a half," she said.

The coach stayed with her, though, and convinced Zinkavich to swap her tennis racket for some pads and to give the game a try. In Zinkavich's words, the coach then proceeded "to scare the crap out of" her. She had a senior player who was bound for Duke on a scholarship fire shots at her one after another. "I can't do this," Zinkavich thought.

But she could, quite well as it turned out. She went on to play goalie for Penn State from 2000-03. She racked up eight shutouts in 2002 for the team that advanced to the NCAA national championship game When the Lions upset No. 6 North Carolina 2-1 that season, she set a Bigler Field record with ten saves.

Despite Zinkavich's decided aversion to running of any sort, she became one of the most fit players on the team. Before her senior season, she said she "kind of breezed through" the exceptionally grueling pre-season. And how was that? Intense running on her own: "I came in in amazing shape because I want to win."

When her playing days ended, Zinkavich went into coaching, spending six seasons at Penn State as an assistant before moving to Virginia. Her life had swung full circle; she had become the one responsible for making sure the players got their running in.

Every morning you hit the ground running as you leave home and re-enter the rat race. You run errands; you run though a presentation; you give someone a run for his money; you always want to be in the running and never run-of-the-mill.

You're always running toward something, such as your goals, or away from something, such as your past. Many of us foolishly spend much of our lives attempting to run away from God, the purposes he has for us, and the blessings he is waiting to give us.

No matter how hard or how far you run, though, you can never outrun yourself or God. God keeps pace with you, calling you in the short run to take care of the long run by falling to your knees and running for your life — to Jesus — just as Peter and the other disciple ran that first Easter morning.

On your knees, you run all the way to glory.

*I never get tired of running. The ball ain't that heavy.*
— *Herschel Walker*

**You can run to eternity by going to your knees.**

# GET THE WORD OUT

**Read Mark 1:21-28.**

*"News about him spread quickly over the whole region"*
*(v. 28).*

**T**he greatest recruit Joe Paterno ever nabbed learned early on that it pays to advertise.

When Paterno was an assistant coach for Rip Engle, one of his duties was the checking of players in and out of study hall. Along the way, he was struck by a freshman English literature honors student who spent a great deal of time at the library conducting research. The courtship approach of the scholarly coach who had once planned on attending law school after he graduated from Brown was somewhat lacking in old-fashioned romance. "He [kept] telling me to keep studying," that freshman recalled. "I said, 'Fine, mister, mister, mister.'"

"Yeah, I was being recruited. I didn't know it," she said. "It took awhile." The coach's persistence — and most assuredly not his technique — eventually landed the most important recruit of his life. He married Suzanne Pohland in 1962, the year she graduated from Penn State.

As a literature major, Sue Paterno always understood and appreciated the power that words have. She used that power once to solve a transportation problem.

Even in the early days of her husband's career, she tried to make every game, though she didn't have a car. During the 1967 season

# NITTANY LIONS

— her husband's second as head coach — she teamed with Sandra Welsh, wife of the backfield coach, George Welsh, to advertise on the local radio station for a ride to the Navy game in Annapolis. They didn't give their names, and two students answered the ad.

"Boy, were they impressed when they found out who we were," Sue recalled. "They even bought our lunch. Good thing, too; we only had five dollars between us."

Commercials, advertisements, pitches, and promotions for products and services inundate us. Turn on your computer and ads pop up automatically. At a NASCAR race, decals cover the cars and the drivers' uniforms. TV, radio, newspapers, billboards, magazines — everyone's trying to get the word out.

Jesus was no different in that he used the most effective and efficient means of advertising he had at his disposal to spread his message of salvation and hope among the masses. That was word of mouth. In his ministry, Jesus didn't isolate himself; instead, he moved from town to town among the common people, preaching, teaching, and healing. Those who encountered Jesus then told others about their experience, thus spreading the word about the good news.

Almost two millennia later, nothing's really changed. Speaking to someone else about Jesus remains the best way to get the word out, and the best advertisement of all is a changed life.

*As soon as I heard [the ad] on the air, I wanted to crawl into a hole, but it was too late then.*
*— Sue Paterno on her successful ad campaign*

**The best advertising for Jesus is word of mouth, telling others what he has done for you.**

# TO TELL THE TRUTH

**Read Matthew 5:33-37.**

*"Simply let your 'Yes' be 'Yes,' and your 'No,' 'No';
anything beyond this comes from the evil one" (v. 37).*

The lie the quarterback told his coach was only a little one, a matter of less than two yards. As a result, though, Penn State kept its hopes for a national championship alive.

On Nov. 24, 1978, for the first time in their 91-year football history, the Nittany Lions took the field as the nation's top-ranked team. A defeat of Pitt would preserve that ranking, complete the undefeated season, and leave the Lions in a position to claim the title on the field. State took the lead with a 3-yard run from Mike Guman and the PAT from Matt Bahr. After that, the Lion offense went as cold as the weather. With only 6:32 to play, Pitt led 10-7.

After a short Panther punt, the Lions moved to a fourth and short at the Pittsburgh 4 with 5:02 left. Just how short they were became quite a bone of contention. Joe Paterno decided to go for the tie and sent the field-goal unit onto the field. He then called a time out to consider his options. He said he wanted to go for the first down, but he couldn't see the ball from the sideline. Just how short were they?

One assistant said four yards. Another said two; a third cast a vote for a single yard. Huddled with his offense, an exasperated Paterno called for "the one man he could trust to tell him the truth." He sent quarterback Chuck Fusina out to take a look and report. Fusina came back and held his hands about a foot apart.

That clinched it for Paterno; the Lions went for it. Fusina pitched to Guman; guard Eric Cunningham, fullback Matt Suhey, tackle Keith Dorney, and tight end Irv Pankey all threw perfect blocks and Guman scored untouched. The Lions went on to win 17-10 and punched their ticket for the national title game.

Only after the game did Fusina confess that the distance for the first down had actually been two yards, not the foot or so he had told Paterno.

No, that dress doesn't make you look fat. But, officer, I wasn't speeding. Coach, we're only about a foot short. I didn't get the project finished because I've been at the hospital every night with my ailing grandmother. What good-looking guy? I didn't notice.

Sometimes we lie to spare the feelings of others; more often, though, we lie to bail ourselves out of a jam, to make ourselves look better to others, or to get something we want.

But Jesus admonishes us to tell the truth, and unfortunately he doesn't include any qualifications. Frequently in our faith life we fret about what is right and what is wrong, but we can have no such ambivalence when it comes to telling the truth or lying. God and his son are so closely associated with the truth that lying is ultimately attributed to the devil ("the evil one").

Given his character, God cannot lie; given his character, the devil lies as a way of life. Given your character, which is it?

*I lied a little.*
— *Chuck Fusina on the distance for the first down*

**Jesus declared himself to be the Truth,
so whose side are we on when we lie?**

# CAN'T GO WRONG

**Read Galatians 6:7-10.**

*"Let us not grow weary in doing what is right, for we will reap at harvest time, if we do not give up" (v. 9 NRSV).*

**M**arco Rivera was determined to do the right thing. Even if it cost him $9 million.

Rivera was a three-year starter at guard from 1993-95 for the Nittany Lions. He was second-team All-Big Ten as a junior and a senior. Sportswriter Ron Bracken called him "one of the two or three best Penn State has ever put on the field."

Rivera joined guard Jeff Hartings, center Bucky Greely, tackles Andrew Johnson and Keith Conlin (all of whom were NFL draftees), and tight end Kyle Brady to form the 1994 group that Bracken called "hands down the best collection of blockers Joe Paterno has ever had on the best offense the Nittany Lions have fielded since 1986."

Rivera was a self-confessed throwback player whose low-key, blue-collar work ethic included unquestioned character and integrity. He carried that character with him into the pros when it led him to do something that for a pro football player was quite remarkable. In 2005, the Dallas Cowboys signed Rivera to a free-agent contract worth $20 million over five years. The agreement also included a $9 million signing bonus.

Shortly after he signed the contract, Rivera suffered a herniated disk during a workout. His options were surgery or retirement.

He was more concerned, however, about the signing bonus, even though it was his to keep even if he never played a down. Rivera offered to return it, saying, "I wouldn't be able to live with myself, just hanging around, collecting a paycheck."

Cowboys' owner Jerry Jones may have been astonished by Rivera's insistence upon doing the right thing no matter the cost, but to Jones' credit, he refused to take the money back. Rivera had the surgery and started for the Cowboys for two more seasons before the back injury forced him to retire.

Doing the right thing is easy when it's little stuff. Giving the quarter back when the cashier gives you too much change, helping a lost child at the mall, or putting a few bucks in the honor box at your favorite fishing hole.

But what about when it costs you — even it's not $9 million? Every day you have multiple chances to do the right thing; in every instance, you have a choice: right or wrong. The factors that weigh into your decisions — including the personal cost to you — reveal much about your character.

Does your doing the right thing ever depend upon your calculation of the odds of getting caught? In the world's eyes, you can't go wrong doing wrong when you won't get caught. That passes for the world's slippery, situational ethics, but it doesn't pass muster with God.

In God's eyes, you can't go wrong doing right. Ever.

*It wasn't right for me to keep the money.*
— *Marco Rivera on offering to return his signing bonus*

**As far as God is concerned,
you can never go wrong doing right.**

# THE FAME GAME

### Read 1 Kings 10:1-10, 18-29.

*"King Solomon was greater in riches and wisdom than all the other kings of the earth. The whole world sought audience with Solomon" (vv. 23-24).*

The quarterback who threw him the ball is more famous, but it is a photograph of receiver Gregg Garrity that "occupies a prominent spot in the homes of thousands of Penn State fans around the world."

That's because Garrity made what in Penn State lore would become known simply as "The Catch." His leaping dive into the end zone to grab a 47-yard pass from Todd Blackledge clinched the 27-23 win over Georgia in the 1983 Sugar Bowl that propelled the Nittany Lions to their first national championship. A photograph of his exuberant celebration in the end zone graced the cover of *Sports Illustrated* and is still today probably the most widely reproduced snapshot in Penn State history.

The Lions led 20-17 two minutes into the fourth quarter with a first and ten at the Georgia 47. Joe Paterno sent out a play that had worked several times during the season. It featured four guys as receivers. Garrity recalled, "We had all seams covered, and someone should be open." Interestingly, all season the throw on the play had not come to Garrity, but this time he was the one who was open.

"I threw the ball as far as I could," Blackledge said later. Garrity stretched and pulled the ball into his chest as he hit the artificial turf. He jumped to his feet "with both arms raised above his head with the ball in his right hand." He had just made "the biggest reception in Penn State history." Photographers snapped away, capturing the moment and making Gregg Garrity famous.

Have you ever wanted to be famous? Hanging out with other rich and famous people, having folks with microphones listen to what you say, throwing money around like toilet paper, meeting adoring and clamoring fans, signing autographs, and posing for the paparazzi before you climb into your imported sports car?

Many of us yearn to be famous, well-known in the places and by the people that we believe matter. That's all fame amounts to: strangers knowing your name and your face.

The truth is that you are already famous where it really does matter, which excludes TV's talking heads, screaming teenagers, star-struck moviegoers, or D.C. power brokers. You are famous because Almighty God knows your name, your face, and everything about you.

If a persistent photographer snapped you pondering this fame — the only kind that has eternal significance — would the picture show the world unbridled joy or the shell-shocked expression of a mug shot?

*When you play a sport, you have two things in mind. One is to get into the Hall of Fame and the other is to go to heaven when you die.*
*— Lee Trevino*

**You're already famous because God knows your name and your face, which may be either reassuring or terrifying.**

# THE DANGER ZONE

**Read Genesis 3:1-24.**

*"So the Lord God banished him from the Garden of Eden
to work the ground from which he had been taken" (v. 23).*

Jose Palacios has nearly died of bacterial meningitis, been saved from drowning in a swimming pool, missed being crushed by an 18-wheeler by inches, and almost been shot at by security agents who detained him at gunpoint. Nothing, however, was ever as dangerous as his bicycle.

Palacios was a member of Penn State's 2000 national championship men's gymnastics team. He was team captain as a senior in 2002 and was honored four times by the College Gymnastics Association as an All-American scholar athlete. His excellent grades didn't come easily; he majored in aerospace engineering.

But as writer Ryan Hockensmith put it, "If there's any time Palacios' intelligence comes into question, it's when he's on that infamous bike. Stationary or non-stationary, dead or alive, friend or foe — Palacios has smacked into just about every person, place or thing in Centre County."

Palacios arrived at State College in 1999 and was on his way to the bookstore — "I swear I was going to buy my books" — when he spotted "that infamous bike" and an unholy partnership began. In his junior season, he estimated he had been struck by vehicles about fifteen times; teammates insisted the total was higher. "He hits them," fellow gymnast Chris Lakeman said.

# NITTANY LIONS

At least twice, Palacios had personal encounters with Campus Loop buses. He once wound up on the hood of a mortified driver's car after a collision. In 2000, Palacios was cited "for violating nearly every bicycle safety guideline in the history of the modern Western world" when an officer flagged him for running through a stop sign at night with no reflectors on the bike, with his hands off the handlebars, with headphones on, and no helmet.

Even if you don't have a malevolent bike seeking to end your life as Jose Palacios did, life is inherently dangerous.

The most dangerous thing you can do in life, however, is to rebel against God by not living the way he has told you to. You may well be what the world considers a "good" person. You're not an adulterer, a thief, or a liar; you don't drink excessively, curse, gamble, litter, or do drugs. You work hard, care for your family, and love dogs and tolerate cats.

But it's not the world's opinion that counts. Despite a sober, responsible lifestyle, you may well be rebelling against God even if you never made the conscious choice to do so. Have you accepted Jesus as your savior? As a result, do you pray, speak Jesus' name to others, read the Bible, attend church faithfully, serve God by serving others, and tithe? In other words, are you living a godly life or a worldly one?

God knows which it is, and if it's the latter, you're sitting right square in God's danger zone.

*I love my bike. I'm not going to stop. I mean, I don't wreck every day.*
— *Jose Palacios*

**Life's greatest danger lies in rebelling against God
by not living the way he has told you to.**

DAY 30

# TEARS IN HEAVEN

### Read Revelation 21:1-8.

*"[God] will wipe every tear from their eyes. There will be no more death or mourning or crying or pain" (v. 4).*

Penn State once had an All-America who detested football but who worked himself to such a pitch for a game that he bawled like a baby.

Charley Way, the original scatback, weighed all of 125 pounds when he arrived at State College in 1917, "but it was 125 pounds of talent." World War I interrupted his playing days, and when he returned to campus in 1919, he was up to 145 pounds.

One of Way's teammates said Way "detested playing football. Head Coach Hugo Bezdek had to have an assistant manager call him from his room to practice every day." Part of that had to do with Way's size, which did not allow him to play the rugged style Bezdek favored. "We practiced every afternoon from 4 o'clock until after dark," Way recalled. "It was quite a grind for a little fellow."

Way, in fact, didn't come to Penn State to play football. His family had little money, so they sent him to State because the tuition was low. When he went out for the football team, it wasn't with a scholarship.

He was a fierce competitor. A Dartmouth player recalled the 1919 game in which three players hit Way at the same time. "The shock felled him like [he was] dead," the player said. "I'll always remember him laying there semi-stunned on the sod . . . as he said: 'I'm hurt a little now but I'll be all right in a minute. And then I'm going to get up and run you big lugs right out the ballgame.'"

Way was so fierce that "he would get worked up to a high pitch sitting on the bench . . . and usually played with tears running down his cheeks and crying out loud like a small child." Tears and all, he led Penn State to an undefeated 1920 season and was named All-America.

When your parents died. When a friend told you that she was divorcing. When you broke your collarbone. When you watch a sad movie.

You cry. Crying is as much a part of life as are indigestion and bad television shows. Usually our tears are brought on by physical or emotional pain, sorrow, or disappointment. But what about when your child was born? When you discovered Jesus Christ? Those times elicit tears too; we cry at the times of our greatest, most overwhelming joy.

Thus, there may well be tears in Heaven; they will, however, serve as evidence of the sheer, unmitigated, undiluted joy we are experiencing. The greatest joy possible, a joy beyond our imagining, must occur when we finally see Christ. If we shed tears when Penn State wins a game, can we really believe that we will stand dry-eyed and calm in the presence of Jesus?

What we will not shed in Heaven are tears of sorrow and pain.

*If I cry, it means I'm too weak to compete in this sport. That's bull.*
    — *NASCAR driver Shawna Robinson*

**Tears in Heaven will be like everything else there:**
**a part of the joy we will experience.**

# DECIDE FOR YOURSELF

**Read John 6:60-69.**

*"The words I have spoken to you are spirit and they are life. Yet there are some of you who do not believe" (vv. 63b-64a).*

Joe Paterno was doubting his abilities as a head coach. Then he made a decision that changed everything, especially the football fortunes of the Nittany Lions.

Paterno was hired as the head coach one day after Rip Engle resigned in February 1966. On Sept. 17, 1966, Paterno won his first game, a "dreadful" 15-7 season-opening win over Maryland. In that game, All-American defensive tackle Mike Reid logged three safeties, still the school record for most in a career.

When the game ended, Paterno couldn't find Terrapin head coach Lou Saban for the ritual congratulatory handshake. Saban called later to apologize. "I didn't come out to shake your hand, but I was so angry," Saban said. "Both our teams stunk; mine just stunk worse than yours did."

"I thought we were great," Paterno said. He also thought, "Boy, what a great coach I am." That feeling lasted only a week; the following Saturday Michigan State blasted the Lions 42-8, sending them on their way to a mediocre 5-5 season.

When Penn State opened the 1967 season with a loss to Navy, Paterno was a troubled man, questioning his abilities. On the bus ride home from Annapolis, though, he made a "dramatic" decision. Six days later against Miami, he gradually inserted five sophomores into the game on defense. Linebackers Dennis Onkotz, Jim Kates, and Pete Johnson and defensive backs Paul Johnson and Neal Smith joined fellow sophomore tackle Steve Smear to become one of the most dominating defenses in school history. They were the backbone of a 31-game unbeaten streak that started with a 17-8 win over Miami.

As with Joe Paterno in 1967, the decisions you have made along the way have shaped your life at every pivotal moment. Some decisions you made suddenly and carelessly; some you made carefully and deliberately; some were forced upon you. You may have discovered that some of those spur-of-the-moment decisions have turned out better than your carefully considered ones.

Of all your life's decisions, however, none is more important than one you cannot ignore: What have you done with Jesus? Even in his time, people chose to follow Jesus or to reject him, and nothing has changed; the decision must still be made and nobody can make it for you. Ignoring Jesus won't work either; that is, in fact, a decision, and neither he nor the consequences of your decision will go away.

Whether it's carefully considered or spontaneous, how you arrive at a decision for Jesus doesn't matter; all that matters is that you get there.

*If you make a decision that you think is the proper one at the time, then that's the correct decision.*
— *John Wooden*

**A decision for Jesus may be spontaneous or considered; what counts is that you make it.**

# AT THE LAST TRUMPET

**Read 1 Corinthians 15:50-58.**

*"The trumpet will sound, the dead will be raised imperishable, and we will be changed" (v. 52).*

Most of the Penn State campus — including many of his teammates — was still in the bed snoring away when Allan Quay (A.Q) Shipley's feet hit the floor each morning. He wasn't getting up before sunrise just to lounge around either; he was on his way to work.

Shipley got into his pre-sunrise routine while he was still in high school. "I like getting up early and just getting it out of the way," he said. "You feel good the rest of the day, feel like you got up and did something."

What Shipley did each morning was prepare himself to play football. He intentionally got up early in high school to beat the sun up for his daily running. "When the sun came out, all my friends were running then and paying for it dearly," he recalled.

When he came to State College in the summer of 2004, Shipley brought his pre-dawn routine with him. Each morning he was up when it was still dark and was in the weight room shortly thereafter, looking at the same faces every morning, many of them his fellow offensive linemen. If any of them were still even slightly drowsy, rock or rap music blared through the Lasch Building weight room. The theme from the movie *Gladiator* was always available for a little extra motivation.

Shipley never needed it. His unflagging penchant for early-morning hard work propelled him into a stellar career at Penn State and eventually to the pros. As a redshirt freshman in 2005, Shipley played on both the offensive and defensive lines. In 2006, he made the permanent move to center. In 2008, he was All-America, All Big-Ten, and the conference's lineman of the year. He won the Rimington Trophy, awarded to the best college center in the country.

Unlike A.Q. Shipley, being roused out of bed before daylight to rush into a weight room for an intense workout may not be a part of your life you'd cherish. You may well agree that the alarm clock is numbered among history's most sadistic inventions.

But one day you will be awakened by a trumpet shrieking in your ear — and you will be overjoyed about it. The Hebrew people of the Bible knew about the good news signaled by a trumpet blast because the sounding of the trumpets announced the start of the great festivals and other extraordinary events. Trumpets blown by the priests controlled and coordinated the march of the people to the Promised Land and reminded them that God watched over them.

The day will come when the last trumpet will sound in the final and true wake-up call. On that day, with that blast, Jesus will summon the faithful to paradise. No one will ever need an alarm clock — or the theme from *Gladiator* — again.

*It's what we live for, eh?*

— *A.Q. Shipley on his pre-dawn workouts*

**God will sound a final wake-up call
at which even the sleepiest will arise.**

# STORY TIME

**Read Luke 8:26-39.**

*"'Return home and tell how much God has done for you.'
So the man went away and told all over town how much
Jesus had done for him" (v. 39).*

Ice cream, poker parties, and Joe Paterno sweating in the car — oh, the stories those national champions could tell.

And tell them they did when the Penn State wrestling team of 1953 — the first Nittany Lion squad to win a national title — gathered at Rec Hall on Jan. 31, 2003, to celebrate the fiftieth anniversary of their triumph, a 9-0 season.

The squad was 7-0 when they took on Pittsburgh, which was riding a 16-match win streak. The Nittany Lions led only 13-12 when Hud Samson wrestled a Pitt football player who outweighed him by more than thirty pounds. Hudson won 2-1 to give Penn State the 16-12 victory.

At a party afterwards at the Samson home, Hud's dad asked the wrestlers what they wanted to eat. "Just ice cream," declared team manager Bill Winterburn. So Samson sent the kids down into his walk-in freezer in the basement "and told them to walk in and take as much as they wanted. They were thrilled." Less thrilled was coach Charlie Spiedel, concerned about his wrestlers making their weight for the next match.

Weight was always on the wrestlers' minds. The season ended with a trip to West Point to take on Army. Wrestler Bob Homan recalled that three of them made the trip wearing rubber suits in an effort to lose weight. Paterno, an avid wrestling fan, was their driver. Said Homan, "Paterno had to sit up front with the heater blazing because we were trying to sweat and lose weight."

The wrestlers stayed in dorms at West Point. Their dorm mates included the Boston College and Boston University hockey teams. "We couldn't get any sleep because the hockey players were up all night playing poker," Homan recalled. PSU won easily 23-3.

So you don't have a host of entertaining stories to tell about the time your team won a national title. You nevertheless have a story to tell; it's the story of your life and it's unique. No one else among the billions of people on this planet can tell the same story.

Part of that story is your encounter with Jesus. It's the most important chapter of anyone's life, but all too often believers in Jesus Christ don't tell it. Otherwise brave and daring Christian men and women who wouldn't think twice about skydiving or whitewater rafting often quail when faced with the prospect of speaking about Jesus to someone else. It's the dreaded "W" word: witness. "I just don't know what to say," we sputter.

But witnessing is nothing but telling your story. No one can refute it; no one can claim it isn't true. You don't get into some great theological debate for which you're ill prepared. You just tell the beautiful, awesome story of Jesus and you.

*Some will be grayer and heavier than in those halcyon days, but all will share stories of what was and what could have been.*
*— Writer Andy Elder on the 50-year reunion of the national champs*

**We all have a story to tell, but the most important part of all is the chapter where we met Jesus.**

# PROMISES, PROMISES

### Read 2 Corinthians 1:16-20.

*"No matter how many promises God has made, they are 'Yes' in Christ" (v. 20).*

Joe Paterno once apologized for not keeping a promise, and in so doing, he set into motion the events that led to the promise's being kept.

One of the emphases throughout Paterno's long career was a melding of athletics and academics, what he called the Grand Experiment, a concept he formulated during his time as a coach at Brown. As a result, scores of his players were named Academic All-Americas. One of those is legendary Penn State and Pittsburgh Steeler linebacker Jack Ham, who said that Paterno was adamant about players' getting their degree.

Thus, a promise Paterno made to Ron Heller's parents during the recruiting process was quite natural. He promised them that he would get their son an education. Heller's priority, however, was a pro football career. He was a two-year starter at offensive tackle for the Lions, including the 1982 national championship team. When he was drafted in the 1984 NFL draft, he completely lost interest in his studies. His last semester he finished with four Ds and an F and failed to graduate.

Heller never thought much about not graduating until a letter came to his parents' home. He remembered seeing tears well in his father's eyes as his dad read the letter. It was a five-page handwritten letter from Paterno apologizing for his failure to get their son a college education. Heller couldn't believe it. "What does he care about me for?" he thought. "I've got nothing to do for him any more."

Because he had made a promise, though, Paterno regarded the failure as his, not Heller's. Moved by his coach's action, Heller went back to school and graduated with a degree in justice administration. The promise was kept.

The promises you make don't say very much about you; the promises you keep tell everything. The promise to your daughter to be there for her softball game. To your son to help him with his math homework. To your spouse to remain faithful until death parts you. And remember what you promised God?

You may carelessly throw promises around, but you can never outpromise God, who is downright profligate with his promises. For instance, he has promised to love you always, to forgive you no matter what you do, and to prepare a place for you with him in Heaven.

And there's more good news in that God operates on this simple premise: Promises made are promises kept. This means that you can rely absolutely on God's promises. The people to whom you make them should be able to rely just as surely on your promises. Make it; keep it — just like God.

*In the everyday pressures of life, I have learned that God's promises are true.*
— *Former major leaguer Garret Anderson*

**God keeps his promises just as those**
**who rely on you expect you to keep yours.**

### DAY 35

# PAYBACK

**Read Matthew 5:38-42.**

*"I tell you, Do not resist an evil person. If someone strikes you on the right cheek, turn to him the other also" (v. 39).*

Penn State head football coach Bob Higgins was the target of so much scorn that when he beat Pitt one season, his wife exacted some payback in a most interesting and unique way: She kicked the editor of an offending publication in the seat of his pants.

Higgins would end his career in State College with ten straight winning seasons including the unbeaten 1947 team, but his early years were rough. In his first nine seasons, he had a winning record only once, 5-3 in 1937, and had five losing seasons.

Taking over in 1930, Higgins was a victim of bad timing as much as anything else. The powers-that-be decided on a "purity" campaign to purge the school of athletic scholarships. "We couldn't even buy a meal for players," Higgins said. Thus, the former two-time Penn State All-America found himself with only a few talented players on hand. That and the Depression "plunged Penn State into one of the darkest periods of its sports history." "We couldn't beat a good high school team!" Higgins lamented.

The Lions were 3-4-2 in 1930, losing 40-0 to Lafayette. They were a disastrous 2-8 in 1931, losing to Waynesburg and Dickinson, and a weak 2-5 in 1932 with yet another loss to Waynesburg.

Higgins was excoriated for his outmoded offense and for using an old-fashioned defense. After a 47-0 blowout loss to Cornell in

# NITTANY LIONS

1939, Penn State's student newspaper pounded him mercilessly. That season ended, though, with the highlight of Higgins' early career, a 10-0 win over Pitt, the Lions' first win over the Panthers in 20 years. After the game, the coach's livid wife, Virginia, vented her frustration by planting a foot right square into the nether regions of the paper's editor.

The very nature of an intense football rivalry is that the loser will seek payback for the defeat of the season before. The desire for revenge is, in fact, what keeps a good rivalry stirred up.

But what about in life when somebody's done you wrong; is it time to get even? The problem with revenge in real-life is that it isn't as clear-cut as a scoreboard. Life is so messy that any attempt at revenge is often inadequate or, worse, backfires and injures you.

As a result, you remain gripped by resentment and anger, which hurts you and no one else. You poison your own happiness while that other person goes blithely about her business. The only way someone who has hurt you can keep hurting you is if you're a willing participant.

But it doesn't have to be that way. Jesus ushered in a new way of living when he taught that we are not to seek revenge for personal wrongs and injuries. Let it go and go on with your life. What a relief!

*When you get licked as often as I did in those terrible 1930s, you get over being a tough guy.*
— *Bob Higgins*

**Resentment and anger over a wrong injures you,
not the other person, so forget it —
just as Jesus taught.**

# WINNER'S CIRCLE

### Read 1 John 5:1-12.

*"Who is it that overcomes the world? Only he who believes that Jesus is the Son of God" (v. 5).*

Joe Paterno bagged himself a Bear on Oct. 27, 2001, when he became the winningest coach in major college football history.

Paterno's march to his 324th career win — which would eclipse Bear Bryant — was an inevitable one, but it didn't come easy. The Lions of 2001 got off to a rocky 0-4 start before a win over Northwestern on Oct. 20 left Paterno tied with the Bear.

Thus, an overflow crowd of more than 108,000 jammed newly expanded Beaver Stadium the next weekend hoping to see history made. The opposition had no intention of cooperating. The Ohio State Buckeyes were a seven-point favorite, and they jumped out to a 27-9 lead less than three minutes into the second half.

But on the second play after the kickoff, freshman quarterback Zack Mills, who hadn't started the game, broke off an option play for a 69-yard touchdown jaunt. After Shawn Mayer recovered a Buckeye fumble, Mills threw a 26-yard TD pass to Tony Johnson. In less than two minutes, the Lions had pulled to within five points at 27-22.

After an Ohio State punt backed the Lions up to their own 10, Mills led the offense on a drive for the ages. They covered the distance in ten plays, the last one a 14-yard pass from Mills to tailback Eric McCoo with thirteen seconds gone in the last quarter.

Penn State led 29-27.

The Buckeyes answered with a 10-play drive of their own that carried to the Lion 17 with 3:31 left. On a 34-yard field-goal attempt, junior tackle Jimmy Kennedy, who stood 6-5, jumped up and batted the ball away.

Joe Paterno was officially college football's biggest winner.

Life itself — not just athletic events — is a competition. You vie against all the other job or college applicants. You compete against others for a date. Sibling rivalry is real; just ask your brother or your sister.

Inherent in any competition or any situation in which you strive to win is the involvement of an antagonist. You always have an opponent to overcome, even if it's an inanimate video game, a golf course, or even yourself.

Nobody wants to be numbered among life's losers, sore or otherwise. We recognize them when we see them, and maybe mutter a prayer that says something like, "There but for the grace of God go I."

But one adversary will defeat us: Death will claim us all. We can turn the tables on this foe, though; we can defeat the grave. A victory is possible, however, only through faith in Jesus Christ. With Jesus, we have hope beyond death because we have life.

With Jesus, we win. For all of eternity.

*I was thinking, 'Block this kick.' It just so happened, I got it. Aw, man, I got Joe No. 324.*

— *Jimmy Kennedy*

**Death is the ultimate opponent;**
**Jesus is the ultimate victor.**

# UNEXPECTEDLY

**Read Matthew 24:36-51.**

*"No one knows about that day or hour, not even the angels in heaven, nor the Son, but only the Father" (v. 36).*

**A**ll the experts knew exactly what to expect from the Penn State men's basketball team. What they didn't expect was a 21-win season and a berth in the Sweet 16 of the NCAA Tournament.

Expectations were decidedly low for the 2000-01 PSU men's squad. As one writer put it in the spring, "the program was a laughingstock." The Lions had gone to the NIT final four the season before, but All-Big Ten forward Jarrett Stephens was gone and forward Gyasi Cline-Heard thought about leaving. Coach Jerry Dunn was investigated by the university for violating NCAA rules. When he was cleared, he checked out the Tulane job. The team faced its toughest schedule in years with no player taller than 6-foot-8 and with no big-name recruits on hand. And the Lions had gone to the NCAA Tournament only twice since 1965.

But in the preseason, the team's three seniors — Joe Crispin, Titus Ivory, and Cline-Heard — declared they were on a mission to put Penn State men's basketball on the map. The team started doing that in November when Crispin and his brother Jon combined for 57 points in beating Kentucky at Rupp Arena. They then beat Illinois at home in overtime and Michigan State in the Big Ten tournament. Both teams were No. 1 seeds in the Big Dance.

But what they did after the win over State was bigger than all that. First of all, they received a bid to the NCAA Tournament. With a No. 7 seed, the Lions beat 10th-seeded Providence in the opening round. That set them up for a date with traditional powerhouse North Carolina, and the Lions surprised the second-seeded Tar Heels 82-74 to advance to the field of sixteen for the first time since 1954. The team no one had expected much of had taken men's basketball "to its highest point ever."

Like those who expected a bad season for the 2000-01 men's basketball team at Penn State, we think that we have everything figured out and under control, and then something unexpected happens. The only thing we can really expect from life with any certainty is the unexpected.

God is that way too, suddenly showing up to remind us he's still around. A friend who calls and tells you he's praying for you, a hug from your child or grandchild, a lone lily that blooms in your yard — unexpected moments when the divine comes crashing into our lives with such clarity that it takes our breath away and brings tears to our eyes.

But why shouldn't God do the unexpected? The only factor limiting what God can do in our lives is the paucity of our own faith. We should expect the unexpected from God, this same deity who caught everyone by surprise by unexpectedly coming to live among us as a man, and who will return when we least expect it.

*I love it when people underestimate us.*
*— Gyasi Cline-Heard on the 2000-01 season*

**God continually does the unexpected,**
**like showing up as Jesus,**
**who will return unexpectedly.**

# THE SCARS

### Read John 20:19-31.

*"'Put your finger here; see my hands. Reach out your
hand and put it into my side. Stop doubting and believe'"*
(v. 27).

The night was the stuff of a situation comedy — except for the
scars it left Alan Zemaitis with.

Zemaitis was a three-time All-Big Ten cornerback and was a
second team All-America as a senior in 2005. He broke the Big
Ten and Penn State single-season records with 207 interception
return yards in 2003.

On a snowy night in January 2003, Zemaitis crashed his car
violently. "I don't know how it happened," he said. He sought
help from two nearby parked truckers "who saw this apparition
walking toward them, nearly scalped, bathed in blood."

That's when the night turned into "a dark comedy of errors."
The ambulance couldn't get to the accident site because of the
snow. "They put the neck roll on me upside down," Zemaitis said.
"I'm thinking this is a nightmare." He walked over and hopped on
the stretcher, but they made him get off — "they said they were
following procedure" — and then helped him back on it.

In the ambulance, one of the stretcher bearers bumped Zemaitis' injured head three times, denying he did it every time. "I was
just trying to survive," Zemaitis said. Because of the extent of his
injuries, he had to be flown by helicopter to a medical center. He

was too tall to fit into the helicopter: "They kept shutting the door on my feet."

At the hospital, the night turned serious again when the doctors stitched him up — "I had lots of stitches." — and drilled a hole in his head to release the pooled blood.

All of Zemaitis' scars from the accident weren't physical. "I had a lot of mental issues about the accident, about life, about how I see things," he recalled. For a while, the smell of an automobile exhaust on campus triggered a flashback because that was the first smell Zemaitis remembered after his car came to a rest.

You've got scars too. Maybe a car wreck left a good one. So did that bicycle crash. Maybe we better not talk about that time you said, "Hey, watch this!" Your scars are part of your life story, the residue of the pain you've encountered. People's scars are so unique and ubiquitous they're used to identify bodies.

Even Jesus proved who he was by the scars of the nail marks in his hands and his side. How interesting it is that even after his resurrection, Jesus bore the scars of the pain he endured. Apparently, he bears them still even as he sits upon his throne in Heaven. Why would he even have them in the first place? Why would he, who had all the power in the universe, submit meekly to being tortured and slaughtered?

He did it for you. Jesus' scars tell the story of his love for you.

*Alan Zemaitis always wore a "Do-Rag"; now he just wears it a little lower on his forehead. It hides the scars.*

*— Writer Ron Bracken*

**In your scars lie stories; the same is true for Jesus, whose scars tell of his love for you.**

# FAIL-SAFE

**Read Luke 22:54-62.**

*"Peter remembered the word the Lord had spoken to him: 'Before the rooster crows today, you will disown me three times.' And he went outside and wept bitterly" (vv. 61b-62).*

**A** dramatic failure directly led to what Joe Paterno called at the time "the greatest football play I've ever seen." It was also described as "thrilling and electrifying."

In 1976, Herb Menhardt was a freshman kicker whose primary passion was soccer; he saw so little action that he didn't even letter. In the last minute of the Iowa game, though, Paterno acted on a hunch and sent Menhardt in to attempt a field goal rather than calling on sophomore starting kicker Matt Bahr.

Trailing 7-6, the Lions were fourth and goal at the Iowa 8. The distance was short, but the kick was brutal. The ball sat on the right hash, the snap from center was low, the holder had trouble getting the ball down. Menhardt shanked it wide left; Iowa won.

That bitter failure led Menhardt to rededicate himself. He studied "performance enhancement and stress management" to help his performance. In 1977 and '78, he concentrated on soccer, not even bothering to practice with the football team in 1978.

In 1979, though, he was the starting kicker, and on Nov. 10 he salvaged the season. Penn State trailed North Carolina State 7-6 in the fourth quarter, two Menhardt field goals providing the only

Lion points. On fourth and 24 with 24 seconds left, four receivers sprinted downfield, and quarterback Dayle Tate hit a wide-open Terry Rakowsky at the Wolfpack 37. One second remained after an incomplete pass.

Menhardt got the call for a long-shot 54-yard kick. He let loose with a boomer that skimmed off the inside right goal post and sailed over the crossbar for the 9-7 win. "This was one of the greatest wins for Penn State," Paterno said.

And it arose out of the ashes of Herb Menhardt's failure.

Failure is usually defined by expectations, which for Penn State's football teams are pretty high. A baseball player who hits .300 is a star, but he fails seventy percent of the time. We grumble about a postal system that manages to deliver billions of items without a hitch.

And we are often our own harshest critics, beating ourselves up for our failings because we expected better. Never mind that our expectations were unrealistic to begin with.

The bad news about life is that failure — unlike success — is inevitable. Only one man walked this earth perfectly and we're not him. The good news about life, however, is that failure isn't permanent. In life, we always have time to reverse our failures as did Peter, he who failed our Lord so abjectly.

The same cannot be said of death. In death we eternally suffer the consequences of our failure to follow that one perfect man.

*When I hit it, I knew it was in the area.*
  *— Herb Menhardt on his dramatic kick against NC State*

**Only one failure in life dooms us to eternal failure
in death: failing to follow Jesus Christ.**

# LOST AND FOUND

**Read Luke 15:11-32.**

*"This brother of yours was dead and is alive again; he was lost and is found" (v. 32).*

**P**enn State once pulled off such an unbelievable win after time had run out that in the ensuing exuberant celebration, a cheerleader lost part of his uniform.

On Oct. 26, 1929, during a 6-3 season, the Lions hosted the Lafayette Maroons. The team's defense was pretty good, but the offense had trouble scoring, managing only seven points or fewer five times that season. Thus, fans weren't too surprised when the Maroons kicked a field goal and apparently made it stand up for a 3-0 win. With only one second left, for some rather strange reason, the Lafayette coach decided to punt rather than run a play. The final whistle blew while the kick was in the air.

Penn State safety Cooper French caught the ball at his 40 and had nowhere to go with three tacklers roaring down on him. But he lateraled to fellow backfield star Frank Diedrich, who went 60 yards for a touchdown and a 6-3 win.

Not surprisingly, "a near-riot ensued" as ecstatic fans swarmed the Beaver Stadium field in wild celebration. The jubilant students carried French and Diedrich off the field on their shoulders. As one newspaper aptly summed it up, "The play left some 15,000 persons dumbfounded."

The collective sense of the Penn State fans wasn't all that was lost in the lively and high-spirited celebration. Varsity cheerleader Izzy Heicklen later placed an ad in the student newspaper, *The Collegian*, that read "LOST — Cheerleader's jacket at game Saturday. Return to Athletic Association office."

Lost along with Heicklen's jacket is any record of whether he ever got it back.

From car keys to friendships, fortunes to reading glasses, loss is a feature of the unfolding panorama of our lives. We win some, we lose some; that's life.

Loss may range from the devastatingly tragic to the momentarily annoying. No loss, however, is as permanently catastrophic as the loss of our very souls. While "being lost" is one of Christianity's many complex symbols, the concept is simple: The lost are those who have chosen to separate themselves from God, to live without an awareness of God in an unrepentant lifestyle contrary to his commandments and tenets. Being lost is a state of mind as much as a way of life.

It's a one-sided decision, though, since God never leaves the lost; they leave him. In God's eyes, no one is a born loser, and neither does anyone have to remain lost. All it takes is a turning back to God; all it takes is a falling into the open arms of Jesus Christ, the good shepherd.

When that happens, what was lost is found.

*A loss gets me eager again.*
— *Tennis legend Chris Evert Lloyd*

**From God's point of view, we are all either lost or found; interestingly, we — not God — determine into which group we land.**

## DAY 41

# KEEP OUT!

### Read Exodus 26:31-35; 30:1-10.

*"The curtain will separate the Holy Place from the Most Holy Place" (v. 26:33).*

They set a school record for wins with 35 and finished third in the Big Ten. Still, though, they were outsiders when the NCAA tournament field was announced.

The Penn State softball team of 1999 went 35-22 and felt they belonged in the tournament for the first time since 1985. It didn't happen. The disappointment drove the team all through the 2000 season.

On May 14, after a 37-17 season — another school record for wins — the Nittany Lions received an at-large bid and a No. 3 seed in the regional in Tempe, Ariz. "We've been shooting for it all year," said outfielder Karen Gulini. "It's been right there in writing for us to look at." She was referring to the three words that were on a white board in their locker room the whole season. They said simply, "One more step."

Once they were in, the players immediately changed their goal from just gaining admittance to the club to proving they belonged in it. "It's not just that we're happy to be here," coach Robin Petrini said. "We're here to play."

On Thursday, May 18, the Nittany Lions proved to everyone they were in Tempe to play. They rallied from a 2-0 deficit against Texas A&M to win 3-2, the school's first-ever regional win. In the bottom of the sixth, Erin Norton led off with a single. With two outs, leftfielder Megan Humphrey drilled a home run to right center to tie the game. After pitcher Tanis Ambelang retired A&M in the top of the seventh, Colleen Kersey drew a one-out walk and Gulini singled. Gina Bianchini laid down a sacrifice bunt, and pinch runner Adrienne Manzo scored from second when the throw at first was mishandled.

Welcome to the club, Nittany Lions.

That local civic club with membership by invitation only. The bleachers where you sit while others frolic in the sky boxes. That neighborhood you can't afford a house in. You know all about being shut out of some club, some group, some place. "Exclusive" is the word that keeps you out.

The Hebrew people, too, knew about being told to keep out; only the priests could come into the presence of the holy and survive. Then along came Jesus to kick that barrier down and give us direct access to God.

In the process, though, Jesus created another exclusive club; its members are his followers, Christians, those who believe he is the Son of God and the savior of the world. This club, though, extends a membership invitation to everyone in the whole wide world; no one is excluded. Whether you're in or out depends on your response to Jesus, not on arbitrary gatekeepers.

*Last year our goal was to get to the Big Ten tournament. This year it was to get further than that.*
*— Penn State softball shortstop Terra Pracht on the 2000 season*

**Christianity is an exclusive club, but an invitation is extended to everyone and no one is denied entry.**

# STILL THE SAME

**Read Hebrews 13:5-16.**

*"Jesus Christ is the same yesterday and today and forever" (v. 8).*

On Sept. 4, 1993, football at Penn State changed forever.

This unprecedented change that overturned more than one hundred years of tradition didn't catch anyone by surprise. After all, it had been in the works for more than three years. On June 4, 1990, Penn State's membership in the Big Ten Conference had become official. The university had decided to place itself "firmly into one of the most respected and prestigious conferences in intercollegiate athletics." It had also surrendered the Penn State tradition of more than a century of football independence.

The idea of giving up gridiron independence wasn't a new one at State College. In the early 1980s, Joe Paterno approached several schools about the creation of an all-sport eastern conference that would include Pitt, West Virginia, Syracuse, Temple, and Rutgers. That proposal fell through, though, when Pitt joined the Big East in basketball. Most of State's athletic teams weren't independent anyway, participating in the Atlantic 10 Conference.

The decision to move into the Big Ten was based almost exclusively on what was best for football since it is the great financial engine that ensures the survival of the other sports. Whether football independence could provide the ever-increasing money the athletic program demanded had become problematic. "We

# NITTANY LIONS

were having a hard time maintaining the kind of program we were accustomed to," Paterno admitted.

And so, on Sept. 4, 1993, the Nittany Lions hosted Minnesota in their season-opening game and their first game in the Big Ten. The new era began quite successfully. State outscored the Gophers 38-20 behind John Sacca's four touchdown passes.

Like everything else, football has changed. Personal computers and GPS systems, smart phones and instant replay on TV, iPods and IMAX theaters — they and much that you regard as essential to and routine in your life now may not have been around when you became eligible to vote. Think about how style, cars, communications, and tax laws constantly change.

Don't be too harsh on the old world, though, because you've changed also. You've aged, gained or lost weight, gotten married, changed jobs, or relocated.

Have you ever found yourself bewildered by the rapid pace of change, casting about for something to hold on to that will always be the same, that you can use as an anchor for your life? Is there anything like that?

Sadly, the answer's no. All the things of this world change.

On the other hand, there's Jesus, who is the same today, the same forever, always dependable, always loving you. No matter what happens in your life, Jesus is still the same.

*I was surprised at how quickly things developed.*
*— Joe Paterno on Penn State's move into the Big Ten*

**In our ever-changing and bewildering world,
Jesus is the same forever;
his love for you will never change.**

# IT'S AMAZING!

**Read: Luke 4:31-36.**

*"All the people were amazed and said to each other, 'What is this teaching? With authority and power he gives orders to evil spirits and they come out!'" (v. 36)*

It's amazing. It's absolutely amazing." And so it was.

Those words of incredulity that must have been accompanied by a gentle shake of the head were spoken by Penn State's Chris Wright. Even he couldn't believe what he and his teammates on the Nittany Lion baseball team had just pulled off.

North Carolina had it all planned out. On Sunday, May 28, 2000, they'd mosey over to the stadium in the morning and win the NCAA regional in the afternoon just like they were supposed to. All they had to do was beat Penn State once. "I don't know," said PSU third baseman Shawn Fagan. "I guess they figured we'd come on the field and roll over."

Well, the Lions didn't. Playing in their first NCAA Tournament since 1976 and facing elimination with a single loss, the boys from State College went out and pulled off a downright amazing feat they even they weren't sure they could do. "It's unbelievable," Fagan said after it was all over. "I didn't think we'd be able to take two games from North Carolina."

But that's what they did. With three starters missing because of injuries and/or illness, the Lions beat the Tar Heels twice — 6-5 and 10-3 — to win the NCAA Regional and advance to the super

# NITTANY LIONS

regional. The Lions really couldn't be faulted too much for having their doubts. After all, they were 0-3 against North Carolina that season, and one of those losses had come in the opening round of the regional, a 14-5 pounding on Friday.

To make it to the super regional, the Lions faced the daunting task of winning four games in less than 48 hours against some of the best teams in the country, including two victories over North Carolina. That's exactly what they did. Amazing!

The word *amazing* defines the limits of what you believe to be plausible or usual. The Grand Canyon, the birth of your children, those last-gasp Penn State wins — they're amazing!

Some people in Galilee felt the same way when they encountered Jesus. Jesus amazed them with the authority of his teaching, and he wowed them with his power over spirit beings. People everywhere just couldn't quit talking about him.

It would have been amazing had they not been amazed. They were, after all, witnesses to the most amazing spectacle in the history of the world: God himself was right there among them walking, talking, teaching, preaching, and healing.

An amazement to equal theirs should be a part of your life too because Jesus still lives. The almighty and omnipotent God of the universe seeks to spend time with you every day — because he loves you. Amazing!

*I don't think anyone thought we could do this.*
*— Relief pitcher Scott Russo on the sweep of UNC*

**Everything about God is amazing,**
**but perhaps most amazing of all**
**is that he loves us and desires our company.**

# HURRY UP AND WAIT

### Read Acts 1:1-1:14.

*"Do not leave Jerusalem, but wait for the gift my Father promised, which you have heard me speak about" (v. 4).*

The Nittany Lions once had to stand around and wait for the clock to run down even though the thoroughly whipped opposition had already given up and left the field.

Penn State and Ohio State met for the first time on Nov. 16, 1912, in Columbus. The game was violent, even by the standards of the day, and Ohio State and its fans didn't take too kindly to it. Nor did they much like the fact that Penn State jumped out front early and never let up.

On the last play of the first quarter, future hall-of-fame quarterback Shorty Miller scored from 30 yards out, and Penn State led 16-0. Ohio State's head coach adopted the tactic of complaining to the refs about the unnecessary roughness, but the officials ignored his pleas, rightly observing that "there was plenty of rough play by both sides." In the second quarter alone, Penn State's Al Wilson was knocked unconscious and lost some teeth, and tackle Red Bebout was stomped in the face.

It didn't matter; nothing could stop the Lions. With about nine minutes left to play, they led 37-0 after another future hall-of-famer, halfback Pete Mauthe, scored. Ohio State's coach decided his team had had enough, so he led them to the locker room after the kickoff. The Lions naturally began to leave the field too, but the head ref declared the rules required that they remain on the field until the clock ran out before they could claim the win.

The crowd got unruly, though, hurling insults and debris at the players as they milled about on the field. Police finally had to rush the field to protect the players, and the ref conceded, ending the game and the waiting with about four minutes left on the clock.

Officially, the score was 1-0, but State records still claim 37-0.

You rush to your doctor's appointment and wind up sitting in the appropriately named waiting room for an hour. You wait in the concessions line at a Penn State game. You're put on hold when you call a tragically misnamed "customer service" center. All of that waiting is time in which we seem to do nothing but feel the precious minutes of our life ticking away.

Sometimes we even wait for God. We have needs, and in our desperation, we call upon the Lord. We are then disappointed if we don't get an immediate answer to our prayers.

But Jesus' last command to his disciples was to wait. Moreover, the entire of our Christian life is spent in an attitude of waiting for Jesus' return. While we wait for God, we hold steadfast to his promises, we continue to serve the world with our ministry, and we remain in communion with him through prayer and devotion.

In other words, we don't just wait; we grow stronger in our faith. Waiting for God is never time lost.

*I stare out the window and wait for spring.*
*— Hall of Famer Rogers Hornsby on the start of baseball season*

**Since God acts on his time and not ours,**
**we often must wait for him,**
**using the time to strengthen our faith.**

# MIRACLE PLAY

**Read Matthew 12:38-42.**

*"He answered, 'A wicked and adulterous generation asks for a miraculous sign!'" (v. 39)*

Nine seconds left to play. Down by three. And the only open receiver is a former offensive lineman with the nickname Stonehands. The Nittany Lions needed a miracle. What they got was dubbed "The Miracle of Mount Nittany."

On their way to the national championship, the fourth-ranked Lions took on No. 8 Nebraska on Sept. 25, 1982, in an instant classic. The Huskers took a 24-21 lead with 1:18 left, but they had given the Lions enough time for a miracle. "We practice the two-minute drill every day," said quarterback Todd Blackledge. "There was more than a minute left, we had 65 yards to go."

And so they went. Tailback Skeeter Nichols got 16 on a screen pass; flanker Kenny Jackson hauled in another Blackledge strike for 16 more. Then the drive stalled; Penn State faced fourth and 11 at the Cornhusker 34 with only 28 seconds on the clock, but Jackson got loose again and Blackledge found him at the 23. First down. When tight end Mike McCloskey got out of bounds with a catch, the Lions crouched at the two with nine seconds left.

Junior Kirk Bowman came into the game with zero receptions in his college career. He had been a tight end just three weeks after stints at linebacker, defensive end, defensive tackle, nose guard, and offensive guard. "I have the kind of body that can play anywhere, I guess," Bowman said about his position changes. Against Rutgers the week before, he had dropped a perfect pass and thus earned his nickname, "Stonehands."

And Stonehands was the only person Blackledge could find as he faced withering pressure. He let fly, and Bowman reached down and made the catch inches off the ground. Touchdown and a 27-24 win. The Miracle at Mount Nittany.

Miracles — like escaping with minor abrasions from an accident that totals your car or winning a football game in the face of certain defeat — defy rational explanation. Underlying the notion of miracles is that they are rare instances of direct divine intervention that reveal God.

But life shows us quite the contrary, that miracles are anything but rare. Since God made the world and everything in it, everything around you is miraculous. Even you are a miracle.

Your life thus can be mundane, dull, and ordinary, or it can be spent in a glorious attitude of childlike wonder and awe. It depends on whether or not you see the world through the eyes of faith. Only through faith can you discern the hand of God in any event; only through faith can you see the miraculous and thus see God.

Jesus knew that miracles don't produce faith, but rather faith produces miracles.

*All I kept thinking about was Philippians 4:13: 'I can do all things through the Lord.'*
  *— Todd Blackledge on the game-winning drive against Nebraska*

**Miracles are all around us,**
**but it takes the eyes of faith to see them.**

# THE SIMPLE LIFE

### Read 1 John 1:5-10.

*"If we confess our sins, he is faithful and just and will forgive us our sins and purify us from all unrighteousness" (v. 9).*

**W**hen Rip Engle arrived in State College in 1950 as the head football coach, he walked into a precarious situation that well could have sabotaged the program. He handled it deftly, however, by employing a simple formula.

Engle once said he "never expected to be a coach" and that he came "from as far down as people can come." He started out at 14 driving a mule in the Pennsylvania coal mines. He never even saw a football game until he played in one as a freshman in college. When he graduated in 1930, high-school coaching was the only job he could get.

After a stint as head coach at Brown, he accepted the offer from Penn State where he faced his peculiar situation. The problem was that his hire came with the stipulation that he retain outgoing coach Joe Bedenk's entire staff. Thus, he brought with him from Brown not a full staff as new coaches usually do, but only one assistant, some 23-year-old who had never coached. Guy named Paterno.

Engle realized he had to talk to these holdover coaches and get them on his side immediately. So he called the staff together and told them that he wanted two things from them: their complete loyalty and their willingness to work hard. He told them to go home and talk it over with their wives.

They did, and as Engle put it, "Everything worked out so well." Indeed it did. Engle coached the Lions for sixteen seasons. He had a record of 104-48-4 with never a losing season. And it all started with the simple formula he handed down to his coaches.

Perhaps the simple life in America was doomed by the arrival of the programmable VCR. Since then, we've been on an inevitable and downward spiral into ever more complicated lives. The once-simple telephone does everything but make coffee, and our clothes dryers have more lights than some Christmas trees.

But we might do well in our own lives to mimic the simple formula Rip Engle used to defuse a potentially disastrous situation. That is, we should approach our lives with the keen awareness that success requires simplicity, a sticking to the basics: Revere God, love our families, honor our country, do our best.

Theologians may make what God did in Jesus as complicated as quantum mechanics and the infield fly rule, but God kept it simple for us: believe, trust, and obey. Believe in Jesus as the Son of God, trust that through him God makes possible our deliverance from our sins into Heaven, and obey God in the way he wants us to live. It's simple, but it's the true winning formula, the way to win for all eternity.

*I think God made it simple. Just accept Him and believe.*
— *Bobby Bowden*

**Life continues to get ever more complicated,
but God made it simple for us
when he showed up as Jesus.**

# NIGHTFALL

### Read Psalm 68:12-23.

*"The day is yours, and yours also the night; you
established the sun and moon" (v. 16).*

**N**ight fell just a wee bit early for the Penn State men's volleyball
team. They were, in fact, only one point away from a trip to the
national championship game — when the lights went out.

On May 4, 2006, at Rec Hall, the Lions met the top-ranked Antelopes of California-Irvine for the right to meet UCLA in the finals.
As expected, the match was a thriller. The Lions played some of
their best ball of the season early on as they jumped out to a 2-0
lead and had a match point in the third game. "We had them on
the ropes in Game 3," Penn State coach Mark Pavlik said. The
coach and his players knew, though, that the Antelopes wouldn't
go down easy. "We knew to expect a run," Pavlik said.

Sure enough, UC-Irvine rallied to take the third and the fourth
games. "As much as I hate to say it, I was thinking that better
not be our downfall," middle blocker Nate Meerstein said about
letting the match point slip away. "Irvine's not a team that you
can mess around with," declared hitter Matt Proper. In the fifth
game, "We had to start right off the bat, especially when it's to 15."

That's exactly what the Nittany Lions did as they jumped out to
a quick 3-0 lead in the deciding game. They never trailed, though
the Antelopes managed a tie at 12 and at 13. When freshman Max
Holt buried a kill from the middle for a 14-13 match point, Irvine

called a time out.

That's when the lights in Rec Hall did exactly what they were programmed to do. Eleven p.m. arrived and some of them went out, effectively leaving the court too dark for play. The teams and the fans could only wait for about ten excruciating minutes until the room was bright enough for the match to continue.

When it did, Holt turned the lights out on Irvine quickly. He delivered a blistering ace and Penn State had the 15-13 win.

With the lighting expertise we have today, our night games — whether indoors or out — are played under conditions that are "as bright as day." It is artificial light, though, man-made, not God-made. Our electric lights can only illumine a portion of God's night; they can never chase it away. And they can fail, plunging players and fans alike into the night's darkness such as happened to Penn State back in 2006.

The night, like the day, is a gift from God to be enjoyed, to function as a necessary part of our lives. The night is a part of God's plan for creation and a natural cycle that includes activity and rest.

The world is different at nightfall. Whether we admire a stunning sunset, are dazzled by fireflies, or simply find solace in the descending quiet, the night reminds us of the variety of God's creation and the need the creation has for constant renewal.

*When we lost I couldn't sleep at night. When we win I can't sleep at night. But when you win, you wake up feeling better.*
*— Baseball manager Joe Torre*

**Like the day, night is part of both the beauty
and the order of God's creation.**

## DAY 48

# TOLD YOU SO

**Read Matthew 24:15-31.**

*"See, I have told you ahead of time" (v. 25).*

It was a bad idea and Levi Brown wanted no part of it. Nope. No way." In the end, though, even he had to admit they told him so.

Brown came to State College in 2002 as a defensive lineman, "and he was going to be one when he left. Period." He spent his first season just as he had expected and wanted: as a redshirted defensive lineman. All year long, though, especially in the spring, his teammates — not his coaches — began to suggest he ought to consider a change. "A lot of the offensive guys were talking to me," Brown said. "'You're coming to offense. It's just a matter of time.' They were waiting for me." Brown dismissed it as meaningless talk; he wasn't the least bit interested.

Then one day before the opening of preseason drills, a couple of the Lion coaches told him he had great ability and they would find him a place to play. To Brown, that still meant defense. "My hopes and dreams were to play defense." But then Joe Paterno got into the act, seeing what Brown's teammates and the coaches saw: He was better suited to offense. Paterno ordered the change, and Brown didn't like it one bit. They told me "where I had to play and I had no choice. I was thinking, 'I don't want to do this. Who do you think you are, telling me where I have to play?'"

The fairy-tale story would say that everything worked out right away — but it didn't. Brown's life went "from a field of dreams to a field of screams." He started all twelve games in 2003 at tackle, and the offensive line drew a lot of heat for the bad season. By Brown's junior season, though, the Lions were back, winning the Big Ten championship. Brown was All-Big Ten as a junior and as a senior. He was the fifth overall player taken in the 2007 draft.

And did he ever admit everyone else was right? During the 2005 season, he was asked if he would return to defense if he got the chance. "Right now, I'd have to turn it down," he said. "I might not love offense, but I like it." They told him so.

Don't you just hate it in when somebody says, "I told you so"? That means the other person was right and you were wrong; that other person has spoken the truth. You could have listened to that know-it-all in the first place, but then you would have lost the chance yourself to crow, "I told you so."

In our pluralistic age and society, many view truth as relative, meaning absolute truth does not exist. All belief systems have equal value and merit. But this is a ghastly, dangerous fallacy because it ignores the truth that God proclaimed in the presence and words of Jesus.

In speaking the truth, Jesus told everybody exactly what he was going to do: come back and take his faithful with him. Those who don't listen or who don't believe will be left behind with those four awful words, "I told you so," ringing in their ears and wringing their souls.

*I believe in Joe and he believed in me.*
  — *Levi Brown on what convinced him to make the switch to offense*

**Jesus matter-of-factly told us what he has planned:**
**He will return to gather all the faithful to himself.**

# REVELATION

### Read Isaiah 53.

*"But he was pierced for our transgressions, he was crushed for our iniquities; the punishment that brought us peace was upon him, and by his wounds we are healed"* (v. 5).

**W**e're a year away from a national championship." So declared Pitt head coach Jackie Sherrill in the summer of 1981. That winter, the Nittany Lions were quite happy to reveal him as a prophet.

As the season rolled on, however, Sherrill appeared to be in error. His team bulldozed one opponent after another on the way to a No. 1 ranking. His quarterback was the second-most efficient thrower in the country, and the Pitt defense was statistically the best in the nation.

Sherrill well understood, however, that his team wasn't necessarily a year ahead of schedule. Pitt played what could kindly be described as a weak schedule, one that included teams such as Cincinnati, Rutgers, and Army during a period when they weren't exactly powerhouses. Florida State, which finished at a mediocre 6-5, "was the only first-rate opponent" the Panthers had played.

The Nittany Lions of 1981 weren't a bunch of slouches, having spent some time atop the national rankings themselves. When they traveled to Pittsburgh for the season finale, they were 8-2 and ranked 11th in the nation. Not even Sherrill, however, could

# NITTANY LIONS

have foreseen the carnage Penn State would inflict upon his team. Nobody could have predicted it after the first quarter ended with Pitt leading 14-0 and having outgained State 164 yards to -4.

But the Lions proceeded to score 48 straight points. Todd Blackledge threw for 262 yards, Curt Warner rushed for 104 yards, Greg Gattuso recovered two fumbles, and Mark Robinson grabbed two interceptions, returning one 91 yards for a touchdown.

Sherrill, it turned out, had indeed prophesied correctly.

In our jaded age, we have pretty much relegated prophecy to dark rooms where mysterious women peer into crystal balls or clasp our sweaty palms while uttering vague generalities. At best, we understand a prophet as someone who predicts future events.

When we open the pages of the Bible, though, we encounter something radically different. A prophet is a messenger from God, one who relays divine revelation to others.

Prophets seem somewhat foreign to us because in one very real sense the age of prophecy is over. In the name of Jesus, we have access to God through our prayers and through scripture. In searching for God's will for our lives, we seek divine revelation. We may speak only for ourselves and not for the greater body of Christ, but we do not need a prophet to discern what God would have us do. We need faith in the one whose birth, life, and death fulfilled more than 300 Bible prophecies.

*We have four players who could start on offense for Penn State. They have seven who could start for Pittsburgh.*
*— Jackie Sherrill before the PSU game, perhaps foreseeing the worst*

**Persons of faith continuously seek a word from God for their lives.**

# YOUNG BLOOD

### Read: Jeremiah 1:4-10.

*"The Lord said to me, 'Do not say, 'I am only a child' . . .*
*for I am with you and will rescue you'" (vv. 7a, 8).*

**M**ost contemporary Penn State football fans probably can't recall the time before the program was in the experienced hands of Joe Paterno. Once, though, long before Paterno, the State head coach was a man so young and inexperienced he had to write another coach for help.

"Big Bill" Hollenback was a three-time All-America at Penn, and when he graduated in 1908, he was offered the head coaching job at Penn State "in an era when young players were given such positions." He was definitely young, only 22.

There was a method to what today would seem like madness, though, in hiring such a totally inexperienced head coach. The game was changing rapidly. The forward pass had been legalized, and teams were given four downs to make ten yards rather than three downs to make five yards. "The young fellows who had just graduated from college understood the new type of play better than many of the old coaches, and so they were hired," Hollenback recalled.

He had players who were older than he was, which didn't seem to matter. As one player, Burke "Dutch" Hermann (later State's first head basketball coach) pointed out, "In those days, pep talks were the difference between a winning and a losing football team.

And Hollenback could really inspire a football team."

The young head coach realized he needed some help, so he regularly wrote to the legendary Pop Warner to pick his brains. Warner dutifully replied with all the answers he could.

And this youngster didn't do too badly. In five seasons, his record was 28-9-4. By the time he was 26, Hollenback had coached three undefeated teams.

While the superficial cultures of movies and television seem inordinately obsessed with youth, most aspects of our society value experience and some hard-won battle scars. Life usually requires us to spend time on the bench as a reserve, waiting for our chance to play with the big boys and girls. You probably rode some pine in high school. You started college as a lowly freshman. You began work at an entry-level position. Even head football coaches learn their trade as assistants.

Paying your dues is traditional, but that shouldn't stop you from doing something bold right away, as Bill Hollenback did in being the youngest head football coach in the country. Nowhere is this truer than in your faith life.

You may well assert that you are too young and too inexperienced to really do anything for God. Those are just excuses, however, and God won't pay a lick of attention to them when he issues a call. After all, the younger you are, the more time you have to serve.

*You're only young once, but you can be immature forever.*
*— Former major leaguer Larry Andersen*

**Youth is no excuse for not serving God;**
**it just gives you more time.**

# THE GREATEST

**Read Mark 9:33-37.**

*"If anyone wants to be first, he must be the very last, and the servant of all" (v. 35).*

**W**hat may still be the greatest game in the history of Penn State women's basketball propelled the Lady Lions to No. 1 for the first time in the program's history.

The women were undefeated and were ranked No. 4 on Jan. 3, 1991, when they took on top-ranked Virginia on the road. The game had been circled on the Lady Lions' calendars since the 25-7 team of the season before saw its run end with a loss to Virginia in the second round of the NCAA Tournament. "A bitter, bitter loss to take" was how then-team manager and current assistant athletic director Jennifer James described the defeat.

The first round of the 1990 NCAA Tournament was a strange one in that a scheduling conflict at Rec Hall forced the women on the road. They played Florida State in Tallahassee even though they were the "home" team because they were higher seeded. They wore the white home uniforms, sat on the home team's bench, and were the home team on the scoreboard, none of which sat too well with the Seminole fans. The final score didn't do much to smooth over the relationship; the Lady Lions won 83-73.

In the 1991 clash with Virginia, Penn State took a seven-point lead at halftime despite missing all eleven of its free throws. The two powerhouses battled even for most of the last half. With 13 seconds left, Dana Eikenberg hit to give State a 70-69 lead, but the Lady Cavs scored with four seconds left. Playing on an injured ankle she had sprained in warm-ups, senior Shelly Caplinger nailed a three-pointer at the buzzer for the 73-71 win.

As a result of that "greatest" game, the Lady Lions were No. 1 when the next rankings came out. They went on to set a school record with 18 straight wins and finished the regular season ranked No. 1 with a 28-1 record.

We all want to be the greatest. The goal for the Lady Lions and their fans every season is the national championship. The competition at work is to be the most productive sales person on the staff or the Teacher of the Year. In other words, we define being the greatest in terms of the struggle for personal success. It's nothing new; the disciples saw greatness in the same way.

As Jesus illustrated, though, greatness in the Kingdom of God has nothing to do with the world's understanding of success. Rather, the greatest are those who channel their ambition toward the furtherance of Christ's kingdom through love and service, rather than their own advancement, which is a complete reversal of status and values as the world sees them.

After all, who could be greater than the person who has Jesus for a brother and God for a father? And that's every one of us.

*Jan. 3 lived up to everything we had hoped for in that locker room ten months earlier.*
— *Jennifer James on the 1991 Virginia game*

**To be great for God has nothing to do**
**with personal advancement and everything to do**
**with the advancement of Christ's kingdom.**

# FOR ALL YOU KNOW

**Read John 8:12-32.**

*"You will know the truth, and the truth will set you free"*
*(v. 32).*

President Richard Nixon obviously had no idea what he was doing when in December 1969, before the bowl games, he proclaimed the Texas Longhorns the national champions.

In what was mainly a publicity stunt complete with photo ops, the president decided to name the winner of the Texas-Arkansas game on Dec. 6 college football's national champion. After Texas' 15-14 win, as the television cameras whirred, Nixon trudged to the Longhorns' locker room and presented the team with a presidential plaque declaring them to be No. 1.

The president's overweening desire for publicity, though, left him with a serious public relations problem. The Nittany Lions of Penn State had finished their season on Nov. 29 by routing North Carolina State 33-8. They were 10-0, their second straight undefeated season, and boasted one of the greatest defenses in college football history. With the bowls still to be played, the Lions had every right to claim the national title for themselves.

"Nixon's gesture . . . caused a furor in Pennsylvania." The president realized he had put his foot in his mouth and sought to remove it by offering Joe Paterno and his team a plaque commemorating their long winning streak. The infuriated and exceedingly blunt coach would have none of it. When a White House official called, he said, "You tell the president to take that trophy and shove it," and hung up.

Paterno may have eventually forgiven the president for his uninformed grandstanding, but he never forgot it, declaring that what Nixon had done "deprived some kids of the opportunity to be called national champions."

Unlike President Nixon and his view of college football in 1969, you may know the score, but there's still much you just flat don't know. Maybe it's the formula for the area of a cylinder or the date of the signing of the Treaty of Versailles. You may not know how paper is made from trees. Or how toothpaste gets into the tube. And can you honestly say you know how the opposite sex thinks?

Despite your ignorance about certain subjects, you manage quite well because what you don't know generally doesn't hurt you too much. In certain aspects of your life, though, ignorance is anything but harmless. Imagine, for instance, the consequence of not knowing how to do your job. Or of getting behind the wheel without knowing how to drive a car.

And in your faith life, what you don't know can have awful and eternal consequences. To willfully choose not to know Jesus is to be condemned to an eternity apart from God. When it comes to Jesus, knowing the truth sets you free while ignoring the truth enslaves you.

*I'd like to know how could the president know so little about Watergate in 1973 and so much about college football in 1969?*
*— Joe Paterno*

**What you don't know may not hurt you**
**except when it comes to Jesus.**

# IN GOD'S OWN TIME

**Read James 5:7-12.**

*"Be patient, then, brothers, until the Lord's coming" (v. 7).*

The fans were probably a little restless at halftime, but the Lions were quite cool and calm. They were, in fact, a patient bunch.

The Northwestern game of Oct. 31, 2009, was clearly what is known as a "trap" game. The 7-1 Lions were the favorites; the Wildcats were only 5-3. But the game was on the road; the annual slugfest against Ohio State was next up for Penn State. Moreover, Northwestern was not a bad football team. "I don't think we quite realized how good they are offensively," Joe Paterno said. Sure enough, Northwestern rolled up 246 yards offense in the first half and led 13-10 at halftime.

Still, a patient confidence reigned in the Lion locker room at the break. Defensive end Jerome Hayes demonstrated that attitude when he said that the Penn State players knew they would be "able to come out in the second half and get into those guys." No panic; just patience that the points would come.

They did, but only after the Lions had to exercise that patience on into the fourth quarter. They tied the game on Collin Wagner's 23-yard field goal. Then quite suddenly came three touchdowns in three offensive plays.

After Northwestern punted, Brandon Beachum bulled his way into the end zone from the two to finish up a 58-yard drive with

12:27 to play. Northwestern went three-and-out. On the first play, quarterback Daryll Clark dropped a deep pass to wide receiver Derek Moye who went the distance, 53 yards. Northwestern ran three plays and had to punt again, and once more on the first play after the exchange, State scored. Tailback Evan Royster burst up the middle for 69 yards and the touchdown.

The patience had paid off; Penn State won 34-13.

Have you ever left a restaurant because the server didn't take your order quickly enough? Complained at your doctor's office about how long you had to wait? Wondered how much longer a sermon was going to last?

It isn't just the machinations of the world with which we're impatient; we want God to move at our pace, not his. For instance, how often have you prayed and expected — indeed, demanded — an immediate answer from God? And aren't Christians the world over impatient for the glorious day when Jesus will return and set everything right? We're in a hurry but God obviously isn't.

As rare as it seems to be, patience is nevertheless included among the likes of gentleness, humility, kindness, and compassion as attributes of a Christian.

God expects us to be patient. He knows what he's doing, he is in control, and his will shall be done. And whether we like it or not, it will be done according to his timetable, not ours.

*That whole first half, we knew it was just a matter of time before we started putting points up.*

*— Center Stefen Wisniewski*

**God moves in his own time, so often we must wait for him to act, remaining faithful and patient.**

# TEN TO REMEMBER

### Read Exodus 20:1-17.

*"God spoke all these words: 'I am the Lord your God . . . .
You shall have no other gods before me'" (vv. 1, 3).*

**C**onceding that the task "wasn't easy," on Oct. 16, 1993, *The Daily Collegian*, Penn State's student newspaper, used the occasion of the Lions' 1,000th football game to select the ten "most memorable" games in school history.

Number one was no surprise: the 14-10 win over Miami on Jan. 2, 1987, that won the Lions' second national championship. The defense led the way with five interceptions. (See Devotion No. 2.)

"Joe Paterno was due," the newspaper said about the Lions' second most memorable game: the 27-23 win over Georgia in the 1983 Sugar Bowl that garnered Penn State's first national championship. No. 3 is the 14-7 loss to Alabama in the 1979 Sugar Bowl as Penn State's national title bid fell short by six inches.

The paper's fourth most memorable game is the 27-24 defeat of Nebraska on Sept. 25, 1982. (See Devotion No. 45.) Number five is the equally exciting 15-14 win over Kansas in the 1969 Orange Bowl. (See Devotion No. 87.)

Number six on the list is the Lions' 24-21 win over No. 1 Notre Dame on Nov. 17, 1990. "That was the greatest moment I've ever had in sports," said Craig Fayak about that game. That's because his "moment" came when he kicked a 34-yard field goal with time running out to win the game.

The seventh most memorable game is the 48-14 rout of Pitt in 1981. (See Devotion No. 49.) Closing out the ten most memorable games in Penn State football history of the first 999 games are the 27-0 rout of Ohio State in 1964, the 54-0 blasting of Bucknell in 1887 that started it all (See Devotion No. 1), and the 13-13 tie with SMU in the 1948 Cotton Bowl.

For Penn State fans, these are indeed ten games to remember — at least through the first 1,000.

You've got your list and you're ready to go: a gallon of paint and a water hose from the hardware store; chips, peanuts, and sodas from the grocery store for watching tonight's football game with your buddies; the tickets for the band concert. Your list helps you remember.

God also made a list once of things he wanted you to remember; it's called the Ten Commandments. Just as your list reminds you to do something, so does God's list remind you of how you are to act in your dealings with other people and with him.

A life dedicated to Jesus is a life devoted to relationships, and God's list emphasizes that the social life and the spiritual life of the faithful cannot be sundered. God's relationship to you is one of unceasing, unqualified love, and you are to mirror that divine love in your relationships with others.

In case you forget, you have a list.

*Society today treats the Ten Commandments as if they were the ten suggestions. Never compromise on right or wrong.*
*— College baseball coach Gordie Gillespie*

**God's list is a set of instructions on how you are to conduct yourself with other people and with him.**

# THE REWARD

### Read 1 Corinthians 3:10-17.

*"If what he has built survives, he will receive his reward"*
*(v. 14).*

After twenty years at Penn State as head basketball coach, more than 450 wins, and "enough league championships to fill all of her fingers with rings," Rene Portland finally got her just reward.

On Monday, March 27, 2000, the Lady Lions crushed Louisiana Tech 86-65 to send Portland and Penn State to the Final Four for the first time in school history.

"Coach told us that this was going to be the class that was going to get her there. And here we are," said Helen Darling of herself and fellow seniors Andrea Garner and Marissa Graby. Darling was a major reason for the Lions' most successful season ever. The four-year starting point guard was the Big Ten Player of the Year in 2000, a first for the Lions. At the time, she was the only Lady Lion in history to score 1,000 points, dish out 600 assists, and pull down 500 rebounds. Darling's last-second heroics, in fact, sent the Lady Lions to the regional finals. With 12.6 seconds left, she put back an offensive rebound for the winning basket in a 66-65 win over Iowa State.

When the 29-4 Lady Lions met Louisiana Tech in the regional finals, they met the team that had ousted them from the NCAA tourney the season before. This time, it was no contest. On her way to becoming Penn State's career leader in three-point baskets, junior Lisa Shepherd nailed three treys in a row and led the Lady Lions to a 45-29 halftime lead. She finished with 25 points; Darling and Garner had 15 each.

Darling, by the way, gave her coach a reward she may not have wanted as much as the trip to the Final Four. With exactly one minute left to play and the boxes of Final Four hats and T-shirts showing up on the bench, Portland took Darling out, and they hugged "for a good 10 seconds." "I was just so happy," the hot and perspiring Darling explained, "but I think I ruined her outfit."

We want our rewards now. Hire a new football coach; he better win right away. You want to keep me happy? Let's see a raise and a promotion immediately or I'm looking for another job. Want that new car or big house you can't afford? Hey that's what they make credit for, so I can live the good life without having to wait.

Jesus spoke often about rewards, but in terms of eternal salvation and service to others rather than instant gratification or self-aggrandizement. The reward Jesus has in mind for us is the inevitable result of the way of life Jesus taught. To live with faith in God and in service to others is to move surely — if not swiftly — toward the eternal rewards included in our salvation.

The world's ephemeral material rewards may pass us by if we don't grab them right now. God's eternal spiritual rewards, however, will absolutely be ours.

*This is incredibly sweet.*
> — *Rene Portland on the win over La Tech*

**God rewards our faith, patience, and service
by fulfilling the promises he has made to us.**

DAY 56

# WORK ETHIC

### Read Matthew 9:35-38.

*"Then he said to his disciples, 'The harvest is plentiful but the workers are few. Ask the Lord of the harvest, therefore, to send out workers into his harvest field'" (vv. 37-38).*

**N**ot all of his fans appreciated how much work Chuck Fusina put into being a Penn State quarterback.

Fusina ended his career in 1978 as the school's career passing yardage leader, a record subsequently broken first by Tony Sacca (1988-91) and then by Zack Mills (2001-04), who is still the record-holder. Fusina was All-America in 1978 and won the Maxwell Award as the nation's outstanding player. In 1977, he set school records for completions, passing attempts, and passing yardage. Against N.C. State and its top-ranked pass defense in 1977, he set school records for completions (22) and yardage (315) in a game. He drove the Lions 83 yards in the closing minutes to pull out the heartstopping 21-17 win. "He threw some passes I've never seen a college quarterback throw," said the NC State coach.

Fusina had the natural talent to be a big-time quarterback, but he also worked hard at it. He finished his sophomore season as the starter, but he threw ten interceptions along the way. Joe Paterno said Fusina "had to become more disciplined, less erratic."

So Fusina went to what he called "summer school" to get better. He took a projector home with him and watched game films over and over again. "I'd sit there in the dark and watch myself throwing those interceptions and I'd see what I should have been doing instead, and I'd call myself a dummy," Fusina said. He also practiced throwing with a buddy hour after hour every day.

All that hard work paid off with a great career. Fusina was also one of the most popular Lions ever. He received more than his share of fan mail, most of it from young fans and most of it quite flattering. One kid, however, wrote Fusina that "he saw me play and decided he wanted to be a quarterback because he didn't want to work too hard."

Do you embrace hard work or try to avoid it? No matter how hard you may try, you really can't escape hard work. Funny thing about all these labor-saving devices like cell phones and laptop computers: You're working longer and harder than ever. For many of us, our work defines us perhaps more than any other aspect of our lives. But there's a workforce you're a part of that doesn't show up in any Labor Department statistics or any IRS records.

You're part of God's staff; God has a specific job that only you can do for him. It's often referred to as a "calling," but it amounts to your serving God where there is a need in the way that best suits your God-given abilities and talents.

You should stand ready to work for God all the time, 24-7. Those are awful hours, but the benefits are out of this world.

*My buddy and that projector, they were very relieved when it was time for me to go back to school.*
— *Chuck Fusina on the work he put in before the 1977 season*

**God calls you to work for him using the talents
and gifts he gave you; whether you're a worker
or a malingerer is up to you.**

# FACING THE MUSIC

**Read Psalm 98.**

*"Sing to the Lord a new song, for he has done marvelous things" (v. 1).*

They all sit together and they dress funny -- but it wouldn't be a Penn State football game without them. When it comes to making noise and generally being rowdy, nobody beats Penn State's Marching Blue Band.

More than 300 strong today, the Blue Band began in 1899 with a six-member drum and bugle corps organized by a student, George H. Deike. The group was soon known as the College Band; its first permanent director, Wilfred O. "Tommy" Thompson, was hired in 1914.

In 1913, sophomore Jimmy Leyden wrote "Victory," one of the songs the band plays at every home game. He wrote a second, "The Nittany Lion," in 1919. He "introduced both songs at football games, standing in the middle of the field and singing the words through a large megaphone with a cornet accompanying him."

"The Nittany Lion" is one of the two songs the band plays when it enters Beaver Stadium and marches down the field in the "Floating Lion" formation. The second song is "Fight On, State," which was written in 1935 by Joseph Saunders, a 1915 graduate then living in Atlantic City. He first gave the song to the freshman class, but it was so catchy that it caught on and was soon a favorite of both the band and the entire student body.

# NITTANY LIONS

The first blue uniforms didn't appear until 1923 when the old brown, military-style uniforms were replaced. The blue outfits were issued on the basis of ability and rank. This select group within the larger band became known as the "Blue Band" and comprised the official traveling band. Gradually, all band members received blue uniforms and the "Blue Band" name stuck.

Showing off its versatility and its talent, the band performed at its most bizarre location ever in New York City in 2005. The band became the first-ever college unit to perform at a major fashion show when 100 students marched down a catwalk.

Maybe you can't play a lick or carry a tune in the proverbial bucket. Or perhaps you do know your way around a guitar or a keyboard and can sing "The Nittany Lion" or "Fight On, State" on karaoke night without closing the joint down.

Unless you're a professional musician, however, how well you play or sing really doesn't matter. What counts is that you have music in your heart and sometimes you have to turn it loose.

Worshipping God has historically included music in some form. That same boisterous and musical enthusiasm you exhibit when the Blue Band strikes up at a game should be a part of the joy you have in your personal worship of God.

When you consider that God loves you, he always will, and he has arranged through Jesus for you to spend eternity with him, how can that song God put in your heart not burst forth?

*Fight, fight, fight for the blue and white; victory will our slogan be.*
*— Opening line of "Victory"*

**You call it music; others may call it noise;**
**God calls it praise.**

DAY 58

# A RIPE OLD AGE

**Read Psalm 92.**

*"[The righteous] will still bear fruit in old age, they will stay fresh and green, proclaiming, 'The Lord is upright'"* (vv. 14-15).

**W**e're too old for this. It's almost past my bedtime."

That's what Joe Paterno told *ABC* he said to Bobby Bowden after one of the most anticipated football games of modern times. The 2006 Orange Bowl matched Penn State and Florida State and pitted the two reigning senior citizens of college football against each other: Paterno, 79, and Bowden, 76. Not coincidentally, they are also the two coaches with the most wins in major college football history .

Befitting two grand masters, their teams put on quite a performance, a triple-overtime thriller that finished at 12:58 a.m., long after everyone's decent bedtime no matter their age. The closing sequence of the classic game resembled nothing so much as a chess match in the park between two seniors.

With the score tied at 23 in the third overtime, FSU missed a field goal on its possession, giving the Lions a chance to win it. On first down, Michael Robinson flipped a little swing pass to Justin King for eight yards to the 17. Paterno promptly sent his kicker, Kevin Kelly, onto the field to win it.

Penn State hesitated, though, and called time out to think it over. Paterno changed his mind and sent his offense back onto the field. FSU countermoved with a time out of its own. After all those strategic moves, Robinson ran for four yards and a first down at the 13.

Another running play picked up one yard, and on second and nine, Paterno decided to send Kelly into the game again. This time he stuck with his decision. Kelly drilled the 29-yarder for the 26-23 win, Paterno's first-ever overtime victory.

The careers of Joe Paterno and Bobby Bowden demonstrated quite forcefully that excellence has no age limit. The truth is, however, that we don't like to admit — especially to ourselves — that we're not as young as we used to be.

So we keep plastic surgeons in business, dye our hair, buy cases of those miracle wrinkle-reducing creams, and redouble our efforts in the gym. Sometimes, though, we just have to face up to the cold, hard truth the mirror shouts to us: We're getting older every day.

It's really all right, though, because aging and old age are part of the natural cycle of our lives, which was God's idea in the first place. God's conception of the golden years, though, isn't limited to close encounters with a rocking chair and nothing more. God expects us to serve him as we are able all the days of our life.

Those who serve God flourish no matter their age because the energizing power of God is in them.

*[Two] coaches that don't want their careers to end brought their teams together for a game that seemed as though it would never end.*
*— Writer Jeff Rice on the 2006 Orange Bowl*

**Servants of God don't ever retire; they keep
working until they get the ultimate promotion.**

# GIFT WRAPPED

### Read James 1:12-18.

*"Every good and perfect gift is from above, coming down from the Father of the heavenly lights" (v. 17).*

Penn State's George Audu won the Big Ten long jump title and then gave away his championship plaque — to a fellow jumper from another school.

When the Big Ten jumpers gathered at meets in the late 1990s, a triple jumper from Purdue named Mike Turner was at the center of activity. "He was very sportsmanlike," Audu said of Turner. "Before the competition he would call all of us together in prayer. I felt he not only touched my life but the lives of other athletes."

On April 1, 1999, Turner's career ended when he suffered a devastating injury during warm-ups. The injury was so severe that the possibility of amputation loomed large for a while. Turner eventually needed eight surgeries to repair the damage and will wear a brace to keep his foot in place for the rest of his life.

News of Turner's injury spread quickly through the close-knit jumpers community, and when Audu heard the news, he had an idea. "I wanted to do something to make [Turner] smile," he said. "I wanted to show him I was still thinking about him." So Audu decided to make an unprecedented gesture: If he successfully defended his Big Ten outdoor championship, he would give the plaque to Turner.

Audu won easily, equaling his career record. He then pulled a

Purdue assistant coach aside, told her what he wanted to do, and handed her the plaque. Turner was speechless when the coach told him. "It almost made me want to cry," he said.

Audi tried to keep word of his gift quiet, but it got out. The NCAA later presented him with its Outstanding Sportsperson of the Year Award in recognition of his selfless act of giving.

Receiving a gift is nice, but giving has its pleasures too, as George Audu's selfless gift demonstrates. The children's excitement on Christmas morning. That smile of pure delight on your spouse's face when you came up with a really cool anniversary present. There really does seem to be something to this being more blessed to give than to receive.

No matter how generous we may be, though, we are grumbling misers compared to God, who is the greatest gift-giver of all. That's because all the good things in our lives come from God. Friends, love, health, family, the air we breathe, the sun that warms us, the food we eat, even our very lives — they're all gifts from a profligate God. And here's the kicker: He even gives us eternal life with him through the gift of his son.

What in the world can we possibly give God in return? Our love and our life.

*That plaque would have been nice to keep, to show my children and grandchildren some day. But there are times when you have to give back to people.*

— *George Audu*

**Nobody can match God when it comes to giving,
but you can give him the gift of your love
in appreciation of his gifts.**

# GOOD SPORTS

### Read Titus 2:1-8.

*"Show integrity, seriousness and soundness of speech that cannot be condemned, so that those who oppose you may be ashamed because they have nothing bad to say about us" (vv. 7b, 8).*

The Nittany Lions of 1927 carried good sportsmanship to the point that it may actually have cost them a game.

College football of the 1920s was a rough sport. For instance, "Lighthorse" Harry Wilson, an All-American running back for both Penn State and Army, had a front tooth knocked out in the 1921 Harvard game. He tried to call time out, but didn't get one as someone exclaimed, "We can't stop for a little thing like that!" Later that night at the railroad station in Boston, the referee handed him his tooth.

It was also a time of unprecedented sportsmanship. When the Lions took on Bucknell on Oct. 8, 1927, the Bisons were without the services of their star fullback, Wally Diehl, who had recently suffered a broken ankle. With the game tied at seven in the last half, Diehl decided he needed to play.

The State players realized that they could cripple the Bucknell star on any play simply by laying a good solid lick on his injured ankle. But when Diehl was tackled on his first carry, the Nittany Lion tackler told him, "Don't worry, Wally, we'll be careful of your bad ankle."

# NITTANY LIONS

Each time Diehl carried the ball and was dropped, the Penn State players "actually went out of their way to avoid hurting his ankle." Inspired by their star, Bucknell won 13-7, their first victory over the Lions since 1899.

Said a Bucknell spokesman after the game: "Whether or not Penn State's fine sportsmanship cost them a victory is hard to say. But if it did, the loss was not commensurable with the gift it made to American football." It was one of Penn State's finest moments.

Many folks who would never consider cheating on the tennis court or the racquetball court to gain an advantage think nothing of doing so in other areas of their life. In other words, the good sportsmanship they practice on the golf course or even on the Monopoly board doesn't carry over. They play with the truth, cut corners, abuse others verbally, run roughshod over the weaker, and generally cheat whenever they can to gain an advantage on the job or in their personal relationships.

But good sportsmanship is a way of living, not just of playing. Shouldn't you accept defeat without complaint (You don't have to like it.); win gracefully without gloating; treat your competition with fairness, courtesy, generosity, and respect? That's the way one team treats another in the name of sportsmanship. That's the way one person treats another in the name of Jesus.

*One person practicing sportsmanship is better than a hundred teaching it.*
— *Knute Rockne*

**Sportsmanship — treating others with courtesy, fairness, and respect — is a way of living, not just a way of playing.**

# MATTER OF THE HEART

**Read Matthew 6:19-24.**

*"Store up for yourselves treasures in heaven . . . . For where your treasure is, there your heart will be also" (vv. 20, 21).*

Joe Paterno first went with the money and the prestige. Finally, though, he went with his heart.

In 1973, Paterno received an offer that he couldn't refuse. The head coach and his team were on a hot streak. From 1967 through 1972, they had finished in the top ten five times, been to five bowl games, and had had two unbeaten seasons. In his seven years as the head Lion, Paterno's record was 63-13-1.

Not surprisingly, Billy Sullivan, owner of the then-woeful New England Patriots, came calling. He wanted Paterno to take over his struggling team and turn it around. His offer was staggering for that time: about $1.25 million over five years.

Paterno understood what was being asked of him: that he change both the direction of his work and the philosophy of his life that had led him to be both a coach and a teacher of young men. He also understood what was being offered in exchange for that loss: lifetime security for himself and his family.

So he sat down with his wife, Sue, and drew up two lists, one headed "Go" and the other headed "Stay." The "Go" list repeatedly came out ahead. "Money, Cape Cod, security, continued rural living for the kids, excitement, a tremendous coaching challenge,"

Paterno recalled. "We made the lists over and over. 'Stay' finished behind all the time."

So he accepted Sullivan's offer. The couple went to bed that night secure in their decision.

When Paterno woke up the next morning, though, he wasn't so sure anymore. He carefully reviewed his decision and realized "the only reason I accepted the job — the only one — was the money. I was flattered by the dough."

He decided the money wasn't enough. He went with his heart instead of his head and stayed at Penn State.

As Joe Paterno did when deciding whether to stay at Penn State, we often face decisions in life that force us to choose between our heart and our head. Our head says take that job with the salary increase; our heart says don't relocate because the kids are doing so well. Our head declares now is not the time to start a relationship; our heart insists that we're in love.

We wrestle with our head and our heart as we determine what matters the most to us. When it comes to the ultimate priority in our lives, though, our head *and* our heart tell us it's Jesus.

What that means for our lives is a resolution of the conflict we face daily: That of choosing between the values of our culture and a life of trust in and obedience to God. The two may occasionally be compatible, but when they're not, our head tells us what Jesus wants us to do; our heart tells us how right it is that we do it.

*You went to bed with a millionaire and woke up a pauper.*
*— Joe Paterno to Sue on his change of heart*

**In our struggle with competing value systems,**
**our head and our heart lead us to follow Jesus.**

# PLAN AHEAD

**Read Psalm 33:1-15.**

*"The plans of the Lord stand firm forever, the purposes of his heart through all generations" (v. 11).*

An opposing coach's plan to defeat the Penn State men's basketball team once meant turning the game into a circus. He succeeded in his strategy but not in getting the win.

On March 1, 1952, Penn State and Pitt played a game in old Rec Hall that Panther head coach Red Carlson turned into a personal forum. He detested the zone defense, believing it should be outlawed. He especially despised Penn State's complicated sliding zone defense, invented by John Lawther, who coached the Lions from 1936-49, and employed by his successor, Elmer Gross (1950-54). The defense had proved to be remarkably effective at shutting down Carlson's offense. He decided to put on a game that would illustrate the evils of the zone defense.

Carlson gave the crowd a hint of what was to come when he walked the length of the court before the game throwing handfuls of peanuts to the crowd. "Get ready, you guys," he shouted to the students. "You're going to see a circus tonight!"

They did. The Panthers won the opening jump ball, and the Lions dutifully retreated into their deadly zone defense. Carlson's boys refused to attempt to penetrate the zone or to shoot the ball. Instead, they stood at a distance and passed back and forth. Carlson's plan was obvious: He wanted the half to end 0-0.

# NITTANY LIONS

The crowd gleefully got into the spirit of the night. One woman took her knitting needles out to a Pitt player. Another took a chair onto the court and invited a Pitt guard to take a seat. Two more State fans offered cookies to the Panther players.

Carlson's plan didn't work. Penn State stole the ball a couple of times in the first half and led 9-4 at the break on the way to a bizarre 24-9 win. State's Jesse Arnelle and Jack Sherry were the game's high scorers with all of six points each.

Successful living takes planning. You go to school to improve your chances for a better paying job. You use blueprints to build your home. You plan for retirement. You map out your vacation to have the best time. You even plan your children — sometimes.

Your best-laid plans, however, sometimes get wrecked by events and circumstances beyond your control. The economy goes into the tank; a debilitating illness strikes; a hurricane hits. Life is capricious and thus no plans — not even your best ones — are foolproof.

But you don't have to go it alone. God has plans for your life that guarantee success as God defines it if you will make him your planning partner. God's plan for your life includes joy, love, peace, kindness, gentleness, and faithfulness, all the elements necessary for truly successful living for today and for all eternity. And God's plan will not fail.

*If you don't know where you are going, you will wind up somewhere else.*

— *Yogi Berra*

**Your plans may ensure a successful life;**
**God's plans will ensure a successful eternity.**

# HOMEBODIES

### Read 2 Corinthians 5:1-10.

*"We . . . would prefer to be away from the body and at home with the Lord" (v. 8).*

**D**iamond Spaz" came home to State College on Sept. 6, 2003, but he honestly wished the circumstances surrounding his homecoming were different.

As a sophomore, Frank Spaziani played all four backfield positions in 1966 and expected to back up Tom Sherman at quarterback in '67. But in the spring, the coaches moved him to defense; he became a two-year starter at end and was a key part of the 1968 juggernaut that went 11-0 and won the Orange Bowl.

In the spring of his senior year after his playing days were over, Spaziani popped into Joe Paterno's office for a quick visit. He sported a mustache, which was against Paterno's rules, but he wasn't on the team anymore. Paterno still expressed his disapproval, and when he left the office, Spaziani had some second thoughts about his hirsute face. "So I went downtown to where I got my hair cut and had the guy shave it off," he recalled. "Then I went back to Rec Hall and stuck my head in his office. He smiled, I smiled, and that was it. The facial hair just wasn't worth it."

Spaziani was always a colorful player, hence the origin of his nickname, "Diamond Spaz." Paterno once famously said of him, "Don't get the idea that I like him because he's Italian. I like him because I'm Italian." Spaziani served as the head football coach of the Boston College Eagles from 2009-2012. *ESPN's* Chris Spielman referred to him as a "mad scientist" who "cooks up plays," and Boston College students sometimes sported lab coats in Diamond Spaz's honor.

So when Spaziani returned to State College in 2003 for the first time since 1989, what made his homecoming so bittersweet? He strode into Beaver Stadium as the defensive coordinator for the Eagles, the loyal opposition on that day. "It's a business, it's a job," he said — and his job was to beat Penn State. "But I'd rather be playing someone else," he admitted.

Home is not necessarily a matter of geography. It may be that place you share with your spouse and your children, whether it's Pennsylvania or Boston. You may feel at home when you return to State College, wondering why you were so eager to leave in the first place. Maybe the home you grew up in still feels like an old shoe, a little worn but comfortable and inviting.

God planted that sense of home in us because he is a God of place, and our place is with him. Thus, we may live a few blocks away from our parents and grandparents or we may relocate every few years. We may wind up halfway across the country, but we will still sometimes feel as though we don't really belong no matter where we are. We don't; our true home is with God in the place Jesus has gone ahead to prepare for us.

We are homebodies and we are perpetually homesick.

*Everybody's better at home.*
*— Basketball player Justin Dentmon*

**We are continually homesick for our real home,**
**which is with God in Heaven.**

# PRESSURE POINT

**Read 1 Kings 18:16-40.**

*"Answer me, O Lord, answer me, so these people will know that you, O Lord, are God" (v. 37).*

**W**ith all the pressure of an undefeated season and the hopes of a national championship riding on its shoulders, the Penn State defense rose up and made a goal-line stand for the ages.

"In every unbeaten season there is a moment, a situation, where everything hangs in the balance," wrote Ron Bracken. For the Nittany Lions of 1986 that moment came on a dark November afternoon in South Bend, Indiana. The Lions were 9-0 and ranked No. 2 in the country on Nov. 15 when they took on a 4-4 Irish team under first-year coach Lou Holtz.

The Fighting Irish drove deep into Penn State territory three times in the first half, getting a pair of field goals. On the other drive, Bob White and Don Graham sacked the Irish quarterback, causing a fumble. Linebacker Pete Giftopoulos recovered, and the Lions promptly marched 78 yards for a 10-6 halftime lead.

Notre Dame took the second-half kickoff and moved 92 yards to regain the lead. John Shaffer brought the Lions right back, hitting Raymond Roundtree for a 37-yard touchdown and then scoring on a sneak from the one for a 24-13 Penn State lead.

Midway through the fourth quarter, though, the Irish scored, and with only 2:29 left, they got the ball back, trailing 24-19. They moved to a first down at the Lion 6, and that's where the Nittany

# NITTANY LIONS

Lion defense made a stand.

On first down, safety Ray Isom drilled the Irish runner for a three-yard loss. Then White sacked the quarterback for a nine-yard loss. On third down, Gary Wilkerson broke up a pass in the end zone with a bone-jarring hit. The defense rose up one last time to stop the fourth-down play at the 13, saving the season — and as it turned out, the national championship.

You live every day with pressure. As Elijah did so long ago and the Penn State defense does every game, you lay it on the line with everybody watching. Your family, coworkers, or employees — they depend on you. You know the pressure of a deadline, of a job evaluation, of taking the risk of asking someone to go out with you, of driving in rush-hour traffic.

Help in dealing with daily pressure is readily available, and the only price you pay for it is your willingness to believe. God will give you the grace to persevere if you ask prayerfully.

And while you may need some convincing, the pressures of daily living are really small potatoes since they all will pass. The real pressure comes when you stare into the face of eternity because what you do with it is irrevocable and forever. You can handle that pressure easily enough by deciding for Jesus.

When you make that decision, eternity is then taken care of, and the pressure if off — forever.

*Pressure is for tires.*

— *Charles Barkley*

**The greatest pressure you face in life
concerns where you will spend eternity,
which can be dealt with by deciding for Jesus.**

# HOLLYWOOD ENDING

**Read Luke 24:1-12.**

*"Why do you look for the living among the dead? He is not here; he has risen!" (vv. 5, 6a)*

**R**ocky. *Rudy. Hoosiers.* Great stuff. They have nothing, though, on Andrew Butville's story.

Butville wrestled in high school and wanted to wrestle at Penn State. His coach called PSU's coach, John Fritz; he told Fritz of two kids headed his way: "They're scrappy. They're tough kids." Fritz' roster was full, which didn't deter Butville, one of the two.

Because he wasn't officially on the team, Butville wasn't allowed to run or do any conditioning with the squad. If he were injured, he had to take care of it himself. He didn't get any warmups, so he had to use and to wash his own clothes. But Butville persevered.

He got a break in the winter of 1996 when the wrestling cap was bumped up a few spots, creating some open slots. One of the criteria Fritz used to add walk-ons to the roster was academics. Butville had a 3.5 GPA in mechanical engineering. He was in.

Butville's Hollywood story didn't end there, however. On Jan. 3, 1997, starting 150-pounder John Lange hurt his knee against Fresno State. That opened his spot in a dual meet against Michigan and Michigan State on Jan. 12. Butville lost eight pounds to make the weight and then won a wrestle-off the Thursday before the meet. Once again, he was in.

Butville was up against a two-time Michigan high-school state champion; it was a mismatch on paper that seemed over when Butville sprained his ankle in the second period. Pressed for time, the trainer taped the outside of the shoe. "I was just in a lot of pain," Butville said, but "I didn't want to give up."

He didn't. He won 11-10. Penn State won the match — by one point. Without Butville's win, the Lions would have lost.

The world tells us that happy endings such as Andrew Butville's are for fairy tales and the movies, that reality is Cinderella dying in childbirth and her prince getting killed in a peasant uprising. But that's just another of the world's lies.

The truth is that Jesus Christ has been producing happy endings for almost two millennia. That's because in Jesus lies the power to change and to rescue a life no matter how desperate the situation. Jesus is the master at putting shattered lives back together, of healing broken hearts and broken relationships, of resurrecting lost dreams.

And as for living happily ever after — God really means it. The greatest Hollywood ending of them all was written on a Sunday morning centuries ago when Jesus left a tomb and death behind. With faith in Jesus, your life can have that same ending. You live with God in peace, joy, and love — forever.

The End.

*Who would have thought he would wrestle in a Big Ten dual meet and not only that but win the match . . . with that bad ankle?*
*— Penn State coach John Fritz on Andrew Butville*

**Hollywood's happy endings are products of imagination; the happy endings Jesus produces are real and are yours for the asking.**

# FOOD FOR THOUGHT

**Read Genesis 9:1-7.**

*"Everything that lives and moves will be food for you. Just as I gave you the green plants, I now give you everything"* (v. 3).

Joe Paterno's order to Andrew Richardson to change positions carried with it a rather unusual mandate: eat.

In his mind, Richardson was a tight end. "I thought I was a pretty good tight end," he said. "I liked to catch the ball." Paterno didn't think so. "When we recruited him, I thought he was going to be an offensive tackle," Paterno said. "But he didn't want to hear that." Richardson went to great lengths to avoid shaping his body to fit the mold of a tackle. He spent only what time was necessary in the weight room to keep his weight around 255 to 260 pounds. "He knew that as soon as he got over that [weight], I was going to move him to tackle," Paterno said.

Finally, Paterno exercised his coach's prerogative: He simply told Richardson he was going to be a tackle, no matter what. Richardson went along with the decision, figuring Paterno knew enough football to know what he was talking about.

Big-time college football doesn't feature any 260-pound tackles, however, so Richardson had to gain some weight. His mission was to load up on the carbs. "When they moved me to tackle, I just let [my weight] go," Richardson said. "The weight came on easy; it really wasn't a challenge. You don't skip a meal, that's for sure. . . . Peanut butter-and-jelly sandwiches helped me a lot."

Richardson's mentor was starting guard Tyler Reed. "We hang out, we go out to eat all of the time," Reed once said in explaining an offensive lineman's lifestyle. "We know where all of the food specials are during the week."

Richardson eventually beefed up to more than 300 pounds and won the starting right tackle job as a junior in 2004.

Belly up to the buffet, boys and girls, for barbecue, sirloin steak, grilled chicken, and fried catfish with hush puppies and cheese grits. Rachael Ray's a household name; hamburger joints, pizza parlors, and taco stands lurk on every corner; and we have a TV channel devoted exclusively to food. We love our chow.

Food is one of God's really good ideas, but consider the complex divine plan that begins with a seed and ends with French fries. The creator of all life devised a system in which living things are sustained and nourished physically through the sacrifice of other living things in a way similar to what Christ underwent to save us spiritually. Whether it's fast food, home-cooked, or a piping hot microwaved dinner in a tray, everything we eat is a gift from God secured through a divine plan in which some plants and animals have given up their lives.

Pausing to give thanks before we dive in seems the least we can do.

*I like to say I'm a slim tackle. I don't look like a 370-pounder.*
*— Andrew Richardson, weighing in at 300 pounds*

**God created a system that nourishes us**
**through the sacrifice of other living things;**
**that's worth a thank-you.**

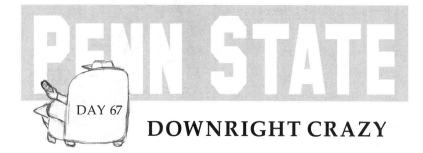

# DOWNRIGHT CRAZY

### Read Luke 13:31-35.

*"Some Pharisees came to Jesus and said to him, 'Leave this place and go somewhere else. Herod wants to kill you.' He replied, 'Go tell that fox . . . I must keep going today and tomorrow and the next day'" (vv. 31-33).*

**D**ave Joyner was convinced his head coach was crazy.

Joyner was an All-American offensive tackle and a captain on the 1971 squad that went 11-1 and buried Texas 30-6 in the Cotton Bowl. In 1969, he was a starter on the line as a sophomore — sort of. "We ran three tackles," he remembered. "[Tom] Jackson and me and Vic Surma would run plays back and forth. So the three of us would play two positions."

That meant Joyner spent time standing next to Joe Paterno on the sideline. He remembered that Paterno would "have his arm around me, and he was getting ready to call plays and he'd talk to himself. He was talking out loud about what he was thinking." As a result, Joyner felt an intimacy with his head coach that few other players could know.

Once, though, that intimacy led Joyner to the conviction that Paterno had basically lost his marbles. One of the highlights of the 11-0 1969 season was the Syracuse game. On Oct. 18, the 4-0 Lions found themselves in deep trouble in New York. They trailed 14-0 in the fourth quarter, and Syracuse had the ball. Joyner was standing in his usual spot next to Paterno.

"And he said, 'They're gonna fumble, they're gonna fumble, they're gonna fumble,'" Joyner recalled. "I was thinking to myself, 'He's crazy.'" Syracuse promptly fumbled, Lydell Mitchell scored, and Franco Harris added the two-point conversion.

With about four minutes left, Syracuse had the ball again, and Joyner stood next to Paterno. "He was saying, 'They're gonna fumble, they're gonna fumble, they're gonna fumble.' And I was really thinking now, 'The guy's lost it.'" Sure enough, Syracuse lost the ball again. Harris scored and State won 15-14.

What some see as crazy often is shrewd instead. Like the time you went into business for yourself or when you decided to go back to school. Maybe it was when you fixed up that old house. Or when you bought that new company's stock.

You know a good thing when you see it but are also shrewd enough to spot something that's downright crazy. With all the wisdom of God at his disposal, Jesus was that way too. He knew that his entering Jerusalem was in complete defiance of all apparent reason and logic since a whole bunch of folks who wanted to kill him were waiting for him there.

Nevertheless, he went because he also knew that when the great drama had played out he would defeat not only his personal enemies but the most fearsome enemy of all: death itself.

It was, after all, a shrewd move that provided the way to your salvation.

*Football is easy if you're crazy.*

*— Bo Jackson*

**It's so good it sounds crazy, but it's not: through faith in Jesus, you can have eternal life with God.**

# GOOD-BYE AGAIN

### Read John 13:33-38.

*"My children, I will be with you only a little longer" (v. 33a).*

**J**oe Paterno gave a pre-game pep talk, the cheerleaders dressed in 1920s flapper and gangster wear, the mascot rollerbladed, and the crowd sang and swayed to "Auld Lang Syne." It was quite a night when Penn State said good-bye to old Rec Hall.

Coach Rene Portland tried to stick to her pre-game routine the night of Jan. 5, 1996, but that went by the board when Paterno asked her if he could talk to her players. Prior to the game, the last-ever at Rec Hall before the move into the Bryce Jordan Center, a choked-up Paterno explained to the players how special the old building had been throughout its 67-year history. It was fitting that Paterno speak to the team because, as Portland said, "He's the guy who let Lady Lion basketball into Rec Hall." When Paterno hired Portland, he promised that her team would have full access to the facility.

Which was something of a mixed blessing. When Rec Hall was built in 1928, no one envisioned women athletes; therefore, the plumbing was designed for men only. The Lady Lion locker room thus included a urinal, discreetly covered by a wooden box.

Paterno delivered on his promise for the 1979-80 season. Before that, the Lady Lions played in the Mary Beaver White Building and used a classroom behind the bleachers as a locker room.

# NITTANY LIONS

After one exciting victory, the players' exuberant celebration included some pounding on a metal chest in the room. The next day Portland got a phone call complaining that the team had broken a skeleton stored in the chest.

"I'm just so excited that our seniors will be getting to play in the Jordan Center," Portland said the night the Lions said good-bye. After all the celebrating and the hoopla, the Lady Lions did the old building proud one last time by stomping Minnesota 77-57.

You've stood on the curb and watched someone you love drive off, or you've grabbed a last-minute hug before a plane leaves. Maybe it was a child leaving home for the first time or your best friends moving halfway across the country. It's an extended — maybe even a permanent — separation, and good-byes hurt.

Jesus felt the pain of parting too. Throughout his brief ministry, Jesus had been surrounded by and had depended upon his friends and confidantes, the disciples. About to leave them, he gathered them for a going-away supper and gave them a heads-up about what was about to happen. In the process, he offered them words of comfort. What a wonderful friend he was! Even though he was the one who was about to suffer unimaginable agony, Jesus' concern was for the pain his friends would feel.

But Jesus wasn't just saying good-bye. He was about his mission of providing the way through which none of us would ever have to say good-bye again.

*It's time to move on.*
— *Rene Portland on the last night in Rec Hall*

**Through Jesus, we will see the day
when we say good-bye to good-byes.**

# AUTHORITY FIGURE

**Read Psalm 95:1-7a.**

*"Come, let us bow down in worship, let us kneel before the Lord" (v. 6).*

The player who was Penn State head coach Rip Engle's all-time favorite routinely disregarded his authority.

From 1957-59, quarterback Richie Lucas established a school record for total offense in a career (2,431 yards). As an All-America in 1959, he set the Penn State single season offense record with 1,238 total yards. He was the starting quarterback in Penn State's win over Alabama in the 1959 Liberty Bowl that forever established Eastern football as the equal of any in the country.

He was nicknamed "Riverboat Richie" because of his flair for doing the unexpected in a game. Engle liked Lucas because of his "gambling ability" and because he liked "to take chances." "He was dangerous at all times," the coach said. "He looked like a choir boy, but had murder in his heart when he played football."

Against the West Virginia Mountaineers in 1957 when he was a sophomore, Lucas forever established his reputation as a riverboat gambler. Instead of punting on fourth and five, he tucked the ball and raced 25 yards for a first down. The play started a touchdown drive, and the Lions were off and running to a 27-6 win. The problem was that Engle had expressly ordered a punt. Lucas, though, had realized that West Virginia's big linemen had been putting pressure on the Nittany Lion punter, so he used the

# NITTANY LIONS

heavy rush to advantage. It didn't really matter much what play his head coach had called.

Not that ignoring Engle's play calling was unusual for Lucas. In fact, Engle was never quite sure what play his quarterback would run when he sent one in. "When [Coach Engle] sends in a play," Lucas once said, "I treat it as a suggestion."

The Lions went 21-8-1 with the riverboat gambler at the helm, so Engle just had to put up with a little flaunting of his authority.

Stand up for yourself. Be your own person. Cherish your independence. That's what the world tells us. Naively, we may believe it and plan to live just that way — until we grow up and discover to our shock that authority figures don't take kindly to being challenged by those under their supervision or direction. Our basic survival skills kick in, and we change our tune: play along, don't rock the boat, be a company person. We become — gasp! — obedient, dampening our rebelliousness for what we regard as a more overarching purpose.

Our relationship with God is similar in that he demands obedience from us. We believe in and trust what Jesus told us as the revealed word of God, and then we are obedient to it.

Obedience — even to God — is not easy for us. It vexes us — at least until we learn that what we surrender in independence to God is meaningless compared to the blessings we gain in return.

*Football is like life; it requires perseverance, self-denial, hard work, sacrifice, dedication, and respect for authority.*
*— Vince Lombardi*

**God seeks our obedience out of a loving desire to provide us with rich, purposeful, and joyous lives.**

# MEMORY LOSS

### Read 1 Corinthians 11:17-29.

*"[D]o this in remembrance of me" (v. 24).*

The Penn State defense remembered. Thus, they came up with a goal-line stand that preserved a thrilling upset of Alabama.

The Crimson Tide was unbeaten and ranked fourth when the largest crowd in Penn State history until then filled Beaver Stadium on Oct. 8, 1983. The Lions were the defending national champions, but after sending eleven players to the pros, they were young. They had stumbled out of the gate at 0-3 before winning a pair of games.

For most of the day, Alabama looked like a juggernaut. The Tide rolled up 598 yards of total offense, but were sloppy with the ball, losing three fumbles and three interceptions. The Lions put together their best game of the season. Freshman D.J. Dozier rushed for 163 yards, junior quarterback Doug Strang riddled the Tide defense for 241 yards and three touchdowns, and Penn State jumped out to a 34-7 lead.

With one second to go, however, the game was in the balance. The Nittany Lions led 34-28, but Alabama sat at the State two with a time out. That's when memory bailed Penn State out.

The whole game in short-yardage situations, the Tide had eaten the Lions alive with the same play, a pitchout to the tailback heading right. Alabama had never gained fewer than seven yards with it. That's what defensive tackle Greg Gattuso remembered as the defense readied itself. End Steve Sefter and cornerback Mark Fruehan also had good memories.

As the Tide offense lined up, they all had the same thought: toss right. Gattuso even shifted one step to his left to gain a head start. Sure enough, it came. The Alabama tailback took the toss, headed right, and found Sefter on the outside, Fruehan in the middle, and Gattuso on the inside. Fruehan met him head-on at the line of scrimmage, and Gattuso grabbed him from behind.

No gain. State win. Because the defense remembered.

Memory makes us who we are. Whether our memories are dreams or nightmares, they shape us and to a large extent determine our actions and reactions. Alzheimer's is so terrifying because it steals our memory from us and in the process we lose ourselves. We disappear.

The greatest tragedy of our lives is that God remembers. In response to that memory, he condemns us for our sin. On the other hand, the greatest joy of our lives is that God remembers. In response to that memory, he came as Jesus to wash even the memory of our sins away.

Through memory, we encounter revival. At the Last Supper, Jesus instructed his disciples and us to remember. In sharing this unique meal with fellow believers and remembering Jesus and his actions, we meet Christ again not just as a memory but as an actual living presence. To remember is to keep our faith alive.

*I could sense it coming.*
— *Cornerback Mack Fruehan on the toss right*

**We remember Jesus,
and God will not remember our sins.**

# CHEAP TRICKS

### Read Acts 19:11-20.

*"The evil spirit answered them, 'Jesus I know, and I know about Paul, but who are you?'" (v. 15)*

**T**he Nittany Lions once pulled off a trick play so daring that it could persuasively be argued that no coach in his right mind would try it today.

Pitt had beaten Penn State six straight times and had not lost a home game in five seasons when the two met on Thanksgiving Day 1919. On the first possession of the game, State halted a Pitt drive at the six. As was typical of the strategy of the day, the Lions immediately went into punt formation.

However, assistant coach Dick Harlow (See Devotion No. 89.), who had scouted Pitt for weeks, had noticed that the Panthers liked to come with a full-blown rush when an opponent punted from deep in its own territory. So the week before the game he created a fake punt and had the team practice it. He decided now was the perfect time.

Instead of punting, fullback Harold Hess tossed a short screen pass to Bob Higgins, Penn State's two-time All-America end, who had pretended to block and was wide open. With end George Brown in front, he turned upfield and romped 92 yards for a touchdown, completing what is still the longest pass play in Penn State football history. Hess had never thrown a pass before and would never throw another one.

# NITTANY LIONS

For some reason, nobody told head coach Hugo Bezdek about the call or the play until the last minute. Not surprisingly, he was a trifle upset. "It sounds OK," he growled, "but next time let me know what's going on around here."

Penn State won 20-0. Said one writer, the trick play "took the heart out of Pitt, who appeared helpless from that stage on. There have been few games in the last quarter century where the Blue and Gold was beaten in the first two minutes of play."

Scam artists are everywhere — and they love trick plays. An e-mail encourages you to send money to some foreign country to get rich. That guy at your front door offers to resurface your driveway at a ridiculously low price. A TV ad promises a pill to help you lose weight without diet or exercise.

You've been around; you check things out before deciding. The same approach is necessary with spiritual matters, too, because false religions and bogus Christian denominations abound. The key is what any group does with Jesus. Is he the son of God, the ruler of the universe, and the only way to salvation? If not, then what the group espouses is something other than the true Word of God.

The good news about Jesus does indeed sound too good to be true. But the only catch is that there is no catch. No trick — just the truth.

*Anyone could have done it. I just happened to be the guy who was supposed to catch the pass.*
*— Bob Higgins on his touchdown on the trick play*

**God's promises through Jesus sound too good to be true, but the only catch is that there is no catch.**

# PAIN RELIEF

### Read 2 Corinthians 1:3-7.

*"Just as the sufferings of Christ flow over into our lives, so also through Christ our comfort overflows" (v. 5).*

Pain from his injuries drove Matt Gaudio from the game he loved. Pain from the separation drove him back.

After playing 54 basketball games for Penn State, Gaudio, a 6-7 power forward, decided to forgo his senior season. He had a good excuse: He had simply worn out his back. "It got to the point," he said, "where it hurt to lay in bed." So in June 1994, a month after back surgery, Gaudio put his Most Inspirational Player Award and his sneakers away.

He went to rehab, just wanting, he said, to be a normal person again, "To not be in pain." He also went to the Nittany Lion bench, serving as a student assistant for the 1994-95 season. He had no interest in playing again. "I didn't want to play in pickup games. I suppressed my feelings toward basketball," Gaudio said.

But as his back healed, those feelings changed. In January 1995, he played a pickup game, "Man," he thought, "this is so fun." He began to plan his comeback. When the season ended with a 21-11 record and a third-place run in the NIT, Gaudio announced his return.

As preseason workouts began, he had had five months without pain, and extensive rehab had made both his back and his legs stronger. He had lost 20 pounds. When the 1995-96 season started, he was there, playing for the love of the game.

Not that the season was pain free. Though his herniated discs didn't bother him, he injured an ankle that finally required surgery so he could keep playing. He actually played in a 69-57 Friday-night win over Tennessee with surgery scheduled for Monday. He scored 13 points and pulled down ten rebounds.

"It's not that bad," he said, but then he added, "There were a couple of times where I didn't want to come down on it hard, so I slid on the floor. I probably made it look worse than it was."

Probably not.

Since you live on Earth and not in Heaven, like Matt Gaudio, you are forced to play with pain. Whether it's a car wreck that left you shattered, the end of a relationship that left you battered, or a loved one's death that left you tattered — pain finds you and challenges you to keep going.

While God's word teaches that you will reap what you sow, life also teaches that pain and hardship are not necessarily the result of personal failure. Pain in fact can be one of the tools God uses to mold your character and change your life.

What are you to do when you are hit full-speed by the awful pain that seems to choke the very will to live out of you? Where is your consolation, your comfort, and your help?

In almighty God, whose love will never fail. When life knocks you to your knees, you're closer to God than ever before.

*With the minutes I played, it'll swell tonight.*
*— Matt Gaudio on his ankle after the Tennessee game*

**When life hits you with pain, you can always turn to God for comfort, consolation, and hope.**

# MAKE NO MISTAKE

### Read Mark 14:66-72.

*"Then Peter remembered the word Jesus had spoken to him: 'Before the rooster crows twice you will disown me three times.' And he broke down and wept" (v. 72).*

Even with a time out, the Nittany Lions totally botched a play from the LSU one as the first half drew to a close. Fortunately, they made up for their mistake and won.

On Jan. 1, 2010, the 10-2 Lions from State College met the Tigers from Baton Rouge in the Capital One Bowl. With only ten seconds to go in the first half, Penn State was camped at the LSU one on third down. The Lions called a time out to be sure they got the play right; it didn't help.

Senior quarterback Daryll Clark wanted to run a play-action fake to the tailback followed by a pass to a receiver out in the flats. The play had worked against both Syracuse and Eastern Illinois during the season. Head coach Joe Paterno wanted Clark to roll to his left and throw a pass into the end zone.

Confusion arose about which play was called. Paterno conceded, instructing the offense to "run his play." But the message didn't get through, and Clark wound up running Paterno's play. The result was a wobbly, incomplete pass.

That mistake loomed big as the game drew to a close and LSU led 17-16, but Clark had one more drive to make in his storied State career. A 12-yard throw to Curtis Drake, a big third-down completion to Graham Zug, and another pass to Zug moved the Lions to the LSU 20. Two running plays later, Collin Wagner kicked the game-winning field goal with 57 seconds to play.

The head coach and his record-setting quarterback could then heave a sigh of relief and laugh about their first-half mistake.

It's distressing but it's true: Like Penn State football teams and Simon Peter, we all make mistakes. Only one perfect man ever walked on this earth, and no one of us is he. Some mistakes are just dumb. Like locking yourself out of your car or falling into a swimming pool with your clothes on.

Other mistakes are more significant. Like heading down a path to addiction. Committing a crime. Walking out on a spouse and the children.

All these mistakes, however, from the momentarily annoying to the life-altering tragic, share one aspect: They can all be forgiven in Jesus Christ. Other folks may not forgive us; we may not even forgive ourselves. But God will forgive us — absolutely and without qualification or reservation — when we call upon him in Jesus' name.

Thus, the twofold fatal mistake we can make is ignoring the fact that we will die one day and subsequently ignoring the fact that Jesus is the only way to shun Hell and enter Heaven. We absolutely must get this one right.

*We ran into a couple of pit stops this game, but we were able to get it done when we needed to.*
*— Daryll Clark on the win in the Capital One Bowl*

**Only one mistake we make sends us to Hell**
**when we die: ignoring Jesus while we live.**

**DAY 74**

# SWEET WORDS

### Read John 8:1-11.

*"'Then neither do I condemn you,' Jesus declared. 'Go now and leave your life of sin'" (v. 11).*

**C**harlie Pittman needed a little encouragement — badly.

Not too much was easy for Pittman when he arrived at State College in the fall of 1966. He found himself stuck as a third-string running back on the freshman team. Even if he broke off a nice run in practice, he received only what he believed to be "luke-warm feedback" from the coach of the freshman team.

Feeling sorry for himself, he called home one day and told his mother how his coach was picking on him. "I don't need this," he said. "I'm coming home." While Pittman's mother may have been sympathetic, his father was not. His dad got on the line and told his son, "If you leave there, you can't come home. If other people are doing it, you can do it. You don't want to work in a steel mill. Stay there and gut it out."

His father's blunt words ended the discussion, but it didn't make Pittman feel any better about his situation. Especially when he had only two carries in his first freshman game.

He was dragging his way to practice, "head glued to his chest," when he passed head coach Joe Paterno and a stranger. "Hey Charlie, how'd you do in the game?" Paterno asked. "I only got to carry the ball two times for 14 yards," the dejected freshman answered. "Well, the next time somebody asks you, tell him you averaged seven yards a carry," Paterno said.

Then the coach did something that forever ended Pittman's thoughts of leaving. Paterno turned to the man with him and said, "That's the guy who's gonna make me a great football coach someday." Pittman later learned the man was an NFL scout.

His worth affirmed, Pittman went on to a sensational career at Penn State. He led the team in rushing for three seasons, was All-America in 1969, and never started in a game that State lost.

You make a key decision. All excited, you tell your best friend or spouse and anxiously await for a reaction. "Boy, that was dumb" is the answer you get. A friend's life spirals out of control into disaster. Alcohol, affairs, drugs, unemployment. Do you pretend you don't know that messed-up person?

Everybody needs affirmation in some degree. That is, we all occasionally need someone to say something positive about us, that we are worth something, and that God loves us. Joe Paterno did that for a discouraged freshman and in the process changed his life and the fortunes of the whole football program.

The follower of Jesus does what our Lord did when he encountered someone whose life was a shambles. Rather than seeing what they were, he saw what they could become. Life is hard; it breaks us all to some degree. To be like Jesus, we see past the problems of the broken and the hurting and envision their potential, understanding that not condemning is not condoning.

*No more calls home.*
*— Charlie Pittman after receiving affirmation from Joe Paterno*

**The greatest way to affirm lost persons**
**is to lead them to Christ.**

# REST EASY

### Read Hebrews 4:1-11.

*"There remains, then, a Sabbath rest for the people of God; for anyone who enters God's rest also rests from his own work, just as God did from his. Let us, therefore, make every effort to enter that rest" (vv. 9-11).*

For Penn State swimmer Kristen Woodring, the only activity she ever loved became the only thing she never wanted to do again. She rescued herself by leaving the water.

Woodring tore the Big Ten up as a freshman in 2001, winning two conference championships and setting two league records. She was the Big Ten Freshman of the Year. "No swimmer at Penn State ever had a better start to a career." Her sophomore season was as successful as she helped the Lions win the Big Ten title.

The success came at a high personal cost, though. "I was barely sleeping. I had constant panic attacks," she said as the pressure to succeed overwhelmed her. "For the first time, I started to question my focus and wonder if it was worth all the time and stress."

During her sophomore season, she began to lose confidence and eventually reached a point when she was so indifferent to her swimming that she didn't get nervous before meets. In October of 2002, she walked into coach Bill Dorenkott's office with a list of reasons why she was retiring from competitive swimming.

Without a scholarship, Woodring held down three jobs to pay her bills. For a while, she found the time away from the pool liberating. For the first time since she was 8, she had time for friends and dates without having to worry about early practices. Over time, though, the desire to return to swimming gradually grew on her. She "swallowed her pride," went back to Dorenkott's office, and asked for and was granted reinstatement to the team.

Reinvigorated by her time of rest from swimming, Woodring returned better than ever, won five more Big Ten championships, and was a first-team All-America both in 2004 and 2005.

As part of the natural rhythm of life, rest is important to maintain physical health. Rest has different images, though: a good eight hours in the sack; a Saturday morning that begins in the backyard with the paper and a pot of coffee; a vacation in the mountains, where the most strenuous thing you do is change position in the hot tub.

Rest is also part of the rhythm and the health of our spiritual lives. Often we envision the faithful person as always busy, always doing something for God whether it's teaching Sunday school, serving at a soup kitchen, or showing up at church every time the doors open.

But God himself rested from work, and in blessing us with the Sabbath, he calls us into a time of rest. To rest by simply spending time in the presence of God is to receive spiritual revitalization and rejuvenation. Sleep refreshes your body and your mind; God's rest refreshes your soul.

*My heart told me and my head told me that I needed a break.*
*— Kristen Woodring on how she rescued her career*

**God promises you a spiritual rest
that renews and refreshes your soul.**

# FAMILY TIES

### Read Mark 3:31-35.

*"[Jesus] said, 'Here are my mother and my brothers!
Whoever does God's will is my brother and sister and
mother'" (vv. 34-35).*

**A**ndy Ryland never knew who was going to be in his family at any one time.

Ryland didn't know whom he might be sharing his breakfast table with, who might be sleeping in the bedroom down the hall, or even what stranger he'd be waiting on to get into the bathroom. "I would wake up in the morning, go downstairs and my Mom would be feeding a baby," Ryland recalled. "I'd just be like, 'OK, who's this?'" That's because the Rylands were a foster family. By the time Ryland grew up, more than forty children had found a safe and loving haven in his household.

In the tight-knit Ryland family in State College, Penn State permeated everything. "My grandfather was the biggest Penn State fan ever," Andy said. "His company (Hoy Transfer) had the contract to haul the football team's equipment to all of the away games." When the adults drank out of the nice glasses at Thanksgiving and Christmas dinners, "the kids had Penn State mugs for their soft drinks. Penn State would be on television." Andy's dad, Terry, was the Nittany Lions rugby coach.

So in 1999 Ryland did the family thing and walked on to the Penn State football team. Unlike most walk-ons, Ryland stuck it

# NITTANY LIONS

out. When he started against Virginia in 2002 and came out of the tunnel after the game, his whole family, down to his aunts and grandmother, was waiting for him, "and they were all in tears."

For the 2003 season, coach Joe Paterno awarded Ryland, a redshirt senior linebacker, a full scholarship. "That was my biggest thrill," he said, his thoughts immediately turning to his family. "That takes a lot of stress off my Mom and Dad. Now that money can go to my younger brothers and sisters."

Some wit said families are like fudge, mostly sweet with a few nuts. You can probably call the names of your sweetest relatives, whom you cherish, and of the nutty ones too, whom you mostly try to avoid at a family reunion.

Like it or not, you have a family, even though it's nothing like the Ryland household with its constantly changing makeup. Your family is God's doing. God cherishes the family so much that he chose to live in one as a son, a brother, and a cousin.

One of Jesus' more startling actions was to redefine the family. No longer is it a single household of blood relatives or even a clan or a tribe. Jesus' family is the result not of an accident of birth but rather a conscious choice. All those who do God's will are members of Jesus' family.

What a startling and wonderful thought! You have family members out there you don't even know who stand ready to love you just because you're part of God's family.

*Your grandfather is smiling down on you.*
*— His family to Andy Ryland after he started the 2002 Virginia game*

**For followers of Jesus, family comes not
from a shared ancestry but from a shared faith.**

# STRANGE BUT TRUE

**Read Isaiah 9:2-7.**

*"The zeal of the Lord Almighty will accomplish this" (v. 7).*

**S**trange as it may sound, Penn State once had an All-American linebacker injured before a game — when he was struck by a teammate's helmet in his own dressing room.

Joe Paterno once said that Greg Buttle was "as good a linebacker as we've had here." In fact, Paterno had Buttle ticketed to play linebacker before Buttle even knew it. "I played tight end, defensive end, split end, punter, and linebacker in high school," Buttle said. When Paterno asked Buttle what position he liked best, he replied tight end. But when Buttle saw that All-American linebacker John Skorupan had just graduated, "I decided to be a linebacker." "You're a pretty smart guy," Paterno told him.

He was also very good. In 1975, Buttle was captain of the 9-3 Lions that played in the Sugar Bowl. All-America that season, he still holds the school record for tackles in a game (24, tied by Bill Banks in 1977)) and in a season (165). He held the Penn State record for career tackles until Paul Posluszny and Dan Connor surpassed him.

In 1974, the Lions were 8-2 and headed to the Cotton Bowl (where they would whip Baylor 41-20) when they hosted Pittsburgh on Nov. 23. The fired-up Lions held a players-only team meeting before kickoff with rousing speeches from All-American defensive end Mike Hartenstine and running back Tom Donchez. During his pep talk, Donchez fired his helmet against a locker. It bounced off and hit Buttle right between the eyes, "leaving him dazed and bleeding."

He shrugged off the strange injury, got himself patched up — though he required six stitches at halftime — and played. "He never missed a signal," assistant coach Jim O'Hora said rather proudly. Buttle did admit that all the action in the first quarter seemed like a dream, moving in slow motion.

Life is just strange, isn't it? How else to explain curling, tofu, the proliferation of tattoos, and the behavior of teenagers? Isn't it strange that so many people actually believe they can meet the "right" person in a bar?

And how strange is God's plan to save us? Think a minute about what God did. He could have come roaring down, destroying and blasting everyone whose sinfulness offended him, which, of course, is pretty much all of us. Then he could have brushed off his hands, nodded the divine head, and left a scorched planet in his wake. All in a day's work.

Instead, God came up with a totally novel plan: He would save the world by becoming a human being, letting himself be humiliated, tortured, and killed, and thus establishing a kingdom of justice and righteousness that will last forever.

It's a strange way to save the world — but it's true.

*Can't we even get through the team prayer without an injury?*
*— Joe Paterno on hearing of Greg Buttle's freak injury*

**It's strange but true: God allowed himself to be killed on a cross to save the world.**

DAY 78

# GLORY DAYS

### Read Colossians 3:1-4.

*"When Christ, who is your life, appears, then you also will appear with him in glory" (v. 4).*

**W**hat is perhaps the most heinous call in the history of Penn State basketball deprived the Lions of a win, but not of glory.

"Just when Penn State basketball had progressed to . . . a level that showed genuine potential for annual" postseason tournaments, the program "was led to what many experts would consider to be the basketball gallows." That would be the Big Ten Conference in 1992 where the sarcastic and smug greeting the Lions heard as they made the circuit that first season was "Welcome to the Big Ten, where there's never an easy win."

It's bragging but it's true. The Penn State men took their lumps as they tried to prove they could compete in the Big Ten. Then in early February, top-ranked Indiana came to a jammed Rec Hall. The Hoosiers had embarrassed the Lions by 48 points in Bloomington earlier in the season. As the students howled and basically went wild and a nation watched in stunned amazement via *ESPN*, Penn State battled Indiana point for point the whole game.

The Lions had a two-point lead when a rebound resulted in a fast break with only twenty seconds left to play. State's Greg Bartram was grabbed from behind by an Indiana player. It was a smart play and not a vicious play. The whistle blew, and the Lions would go to the line "to put a wrap on the biggest upset in school

**156   DAY 78**

history." But the ref saw what nobody else in the building saw; unbelievably, he called an offensive foul against Bartram.

Indiana eventually won the game 88-84 in double overtime. After the game, Indiana's legendary Bobby Knight admitted to State's coach, Bruce Parkhill, that the Lions deserved to win. They had lost, but they had shown the nation they could play ball with the big boys of the Big Ten. It was a glorious night.

You may well remember the play that was your moment of athletic glory. Or the night you received an award from a civic group for your hard work. Your first (and last?) ace on the golf course. Your promotion at work. Your first-ever 10K race. Life does have its moments of glory.

But they amount to a lesser, transient glory, which carries a rueful ache with it since you cannot recapture the moment. The excitement, the joy, the happiness — they are fleeting; they pass as quickly as they came, and you can never experience them again.

Glory days that last forever are found only through Jesus. That's because true glory properly belongs only to God, who has shown us his glory in Jesus. To accept Jesus into our lives is thus to take God's glory into ourselves. Glory therefore is an ongoing attribute of Christians. Our glory days are right now, and they will become even more glorious when Jesus returns.

*On the night when David almost knocked off Goliath, Penn State basketball showed every quality that Big Ten officials had looked for.*
*— Writer Kip Richeal*

**The glory of this earth is fleeting,**
**but the glory we find in Jesus lasts forever —**
**and will only get even more magnificent.**

DAY 79

# NOT A GOOD IDEA

**Read Mark 14:43-50.**

*"The betrayer had arranged a signal with them: 'The one I kiss is the man; arrest him and lead him away under guard'" (v. 44).*

Considering the weather at the time, using sideline heaters for the first time ever certainly seemed like a good idea. It wasn't.

The Nittany Lions met the Oregon Ducks in the second-ever Liberty Bowl on Dec 17, 1960, in Philadelphia. Conditions for the game were somewhat less than ideal, especially for the Ducks. "Oregon never has played on a field even encircled by snow," said head coach Len Casanova as he cautiously eyed the huge drifts that rimmed the field.

What concerned the head Duck was fourteen inches of snow that had fallen recently. Temperatures dropped into the low 30s, and the wind swept through the stadium at 25 miles per hour. A crowd of 16,624 extremely hardy souls showed up in the 100,000-seat stadium. They wound up both frozen and bored.

That's because the weather didn't seem to bother the Nittany Lions one bit as they romped to a 41-12 win. About that weather. The city provided snowplows to help clean up some of the snow. The bowl's founder and executive director confessed he "was out there shoveling with everyone else. It was disheartening to say the least."

In hopes of making the conditions somewhat more tolerable

# NITTANY LIONS

for the players, something brand new was tried: Some infrared lamps were set up a couple of feet over the heads of the players. Expectations were that the lamps would keep them comfortable.

That's not exactly what happened. "Instead, the players turned medium rare," one reporter quipped. "After a quarter or so, they felt as if they had been sitting on the beach in Florida." The lights ultimately made conditions worse for the players by turning the sidelines into one big mud hole.

That sure-fire investment you made from a pal's hot stock tip. The expensive exercise machine that now traps dust bunnies under your bed. Blond hair. Telling your wife you wanted to eat at the restaurant with the waitresses in little shorts. They seemed like pretty good ideas at the time; they weren't.

We all have bad ideas in our lifetime. They provide some of our most crucial learning experiences.

Some ideas, though, are so irreparably and inherently bad that we cannot help but wonder why they were even conceived in the first place. Almost two thousand years ago a man had just such an idea. Judas' betrayal of Jesus remains to this day one of the most heinous acts of treachery in history.

Turning his back on Jesus was a bad idea for Judas then; it's a bad idea for us now.

*Bat Day seems like a good idea, but I question the advisability of giving bats in the Bronx to 40,000 Yankee fans.*
*— Cartoonist Aaron Bacall*

**We all have some pretty bad ideas**
**during our lifetimes, but nothing equals**
**the folly of turning away from Jesus.**

# RESPECTFULLY YOURS

**Read Mark 8:31-38.**

*"He then began to teach them that the Son of Man must
suffer many things and be rejected by the elders, chief
priests and teachers of the law, and that he must be killed"
(v. 31).*

**T**he game was just another challenge for Ohio State. For Penn
State, though, it was something much more: a chance to regain
some respect.

After the Lions logged seasons of 3-9 and 4-7 in 2003 and 2004
respectively, most pundits said the best that Penn State could
hope for in 2005 was at least four or five losses. Thus, despite a 5-0
start that included a 44-14 thumping of 18th-ranked Minnesota,
Penn State didn't garner too much respect across the country. Few
folks considered the Lions to be legitimate contenders for the Big
Ten title.

So when sixth-ranked Ohio State rolled into town for an Oct.
8 showdown, no one was surprised when the 3-1 Buckeyes were
favored. What resulted was one of the greatest games in Penn
State football history. It was classic Joe Paterno: great defense and
kicking and scoring just enough points to win.

After an early Ohio State field goal, the Lions took the lead for
good in the second quarter. A 25-yard romp from tailback Tony
Hunt and quarterback Michael Robinson's 16-yard scramble set
up a 13-yard touchdown run by Derrick Williams. He was sprung

free by a block from right tackle Andrew Richardson. Three plays later, Calvin Lowry nabbed an interception, and three plays after that, Robinson kept on an option and scored.

Ohio State cut the lead to 14-10 with 33 seconds left in the half. The Buckeyes didn't know it, but they would not score again; the rest of the night belonged to the Penn State defense. Linebacker Paul Posluszny led the charge with 14 tackles.

With the 17-10 win, the Nittany Lions were "back in the territory their predecessors took for granted": winning *and* respected.

Rodney Dangerfield made a good living as a comedian with a repertoire that was basically only countless variations on one punch line: "I don't get no respect." Dangerfield was successful because he struck a chord with his audience. No one wants to play football for a program that no one respects. You want the respect, the esteem, and the regard that you feel you've earned.

But more often than not, you don't get it. Still, you shouldn't feel too badly; you're in good company. In the ultimate example of disrespect, Jesus — the very Son of God — was treated as the worst type of criminal. He was arrested, bound, scorned, ridiculed, spit upon, tortured, condemned, and executed.

God allowed his son to undergo such treatment because of his high regard and his love for you. You are respected by almighty God! Could anyone else's respect really matter?

*This was a chance for us to prove we belonged on the national stage.*
*— Safety Chris Harrell on the Ohio State game*

**You may not get the respect you deserve,**
**but at least nobody's spitting on you**
**and driving nails into you as they did to Jesus.**

# THE SUB

### Read Galatians 3:10-14.

*"Christi redeemed us from the curse of the law by becoming a curse for us" (v. 13).*

**H**e was the captain of the tennis team who was on the bench flirting with the girls — until he went in and scored the game-winning goal in a national championship season.

The Penn State men's soccer team won back-to-back national titles with undefeated seasons in 1954 and 1955. The second game of the '55 season was at West Chester University, and on the team that day was Fred Trust. He was captain of the tennis team and was attending Penn State on a combined scholarship for both sports, courtesy of an arrangement cooked up by assistant football coach Joe Paterno. Trust's emphasis, however, was on tennis; he associated little with the soccer team, practiced even less with them, and played none at all in games.

So on this day, Trust was on the sideline flirting with the girls and not expecting to play. The game was tied at two with time running out when Don Shirk, who had played in 1951 and '52 and had returned for the '55 season after serving in Korea, went down with leg cramps. To Trust's complete surprise, Coach Ken Hosterman summoned him to go in.

Trust thought the coach didn't even know his name. "I was just an extra practice guy," he said. When Trust ran onto the field, the coach had to shout at him to take off his sweat suit. "I was a nervous wreck," Trust confessed.

Almost immediately, the ball sailed to Trust, who attempted to get the ball to two-time All-American Dick Packer. He kicked the ball and immediately headed to find his man on defense as he had been instructed. Suddenly, though, Trust found himself mobbed by his teammates. His kick hadn't found Packer at all; instead, it had found the goal and given the Lions a 3-2 win.

A leg injury forced him to give up soccer for tennis, but for one amazing moment, Fred Trust was the soccer team's greatest sub.

Wouldn't it be cool if you had a substitute like Fred Trust for all life's hard stuff? Telling of a death in the family? Call in your sub. Breaking up with your boyfriend? Job interview? Chemistry test? Crucial presentation at work? Let the sub handle it.

We do have such a substitute, but not for the matters of life. Instead, Jesus is our substitute for matters of life and death. Since Jesus has already made it, we don't have to make the sacrifice God demands for forgiveness and salvation.

One of the ironies of our age is that many people desperately grope for a substitute for Jesus. Mysticism, human philosophies such as Scientology, false religions such as Hinduism and Islam, cults, New Age approaches that preach self-fulfillment without responsibility or accountability — they and others like them are all pitiful, inadequate substitutes for Jesus.

Accept no substitutes. It's Jesus or nothing.

*Who are you?*
*— Teammate Dick Matacia to Fred Trust as they celebrated Trust's kick*

**There is no substitute for Jesus,
the consummate substitute.**

# CLOTHES HORSE

### Read Genesis 37:1-11.

*"Israel loved Joseph more than all his children, because he was the son of his old age: and he made him a coat of many colours" (v. 3 KJV).*

Penn State's minimalist blue-and-white football uniforms are a college legend, instantly recognizable. Imagine, if you will, how different everything would be if Nittany Lion athletes wore — of all things — pink and black. They once did.

The Penn State football team was quite the collective clothes horse when it began play in 1887. (See Devotion No. 1). In the two games against Bucknell, the players wore "swashbuckling, tight-fitting, canvas jackets and knee-length pants." They had little or no padding, but they did have "PSC-FB" splattered across the front of the jackets. On their heads, they wore "snug 'beanies.'"

The uniforms, however, were quite drab, and the student body "wanted something bright and attractive," according to George Meek, class of 1890, one of the three students appointed to choose two colors to represent the university. Meek said red and orange were out of the question "as those colors were already in use by other colleges." The triumvirate for some reason recommended pink and black, and the students for some reason enthusiastically accepted the gaudy combination.

Both the school's football team and the baseball team had new uniforms made up that showed off the "bright and attractive" colors. Soon, "the entire campus appeared electrified as pink and black blazers and caps became the new fashion trend of the 80s."

Perhaps fortunately for generations of Penn State athletes, the colors didn't last — literally. After a few weeks of exposure to the sun, the pink faded so badly that the bright and attractive colors turned to plain old black and white. So the committee came up with a second choice, and in March 1890, the student body voted to change the school colors to blue and white. In May, the baseball squad became the first Penn State team to don the new duds.

Contemporary society proclaims that it's all about the clothes. Buy that new suit or dress, those new shoes, and all the sparkling accessories, and you'll be a new person. The changes are only cosmetic, though; under those clothes, you're the same person. Consider Joseph, for instance, prancing about in his pretty new clothes; he was still a spoiled little tattletale whom his brothers despised enough to sell into slavery.

Jesus never taught that we should run around half-naked or wear only second-hand clothes from the local mission. He did warn us, though, against making consumer items such as clothes a priority in our lives. A follower of Christ seeks to emulate Jesus not through material, superficial means such as wearing special clothing like a robe and sandals. Rather, the disciple desires to match Jesus' inner beauty and serenity — whether the clothes the Christian wears are the sables of a king or the rags of a pauper.

*I think I'd feel pretty silly wearing pink and black.*
*— Former Penn State quarterback Tom Bill*

**Where Jesus is concerned,
clothes don't make the person; faith does.**

# NOT REAL SMART

### Read 1 Kings 4:29-34; 11:1-6.

*"[Solomon] was wiser than any other man. . . . As Solomon grew old, his wives turned his heart after other gods, and his heart was not fully devoted to the Lord his God" (vv. 4:31, 11:4).*

I felt like an idiot." So declared Penn State defensive tackle Leo Wisniewski about a play he made that did indeed look awful but was instrumental in a Fiesta Bowl win.

On Jan. 1, 1982, the Nittany Lions met the Southern Cal Trojans for only the second time in history. The first encounter — in the 1923 Rose Bowl — began and ended rather ignominiously for the Lions. The Trojans accused them of intentionally dawdling at the pre-game parade and thus delaying the kickoff by 45 minutes. The game finished in the dark "with reporters in the press box writing their stories by the light of matches." USC won 14-3.

The second match-up was a different story entirely. The Lions romped to a 26-10 win. As inside linebacker Chet Parlavecchio so delicately put it, "We mangled them. We intimidated them. We shocked them." The defense, in fact, set up a touchdown on the game's first play. USC's Heisman-Trophy winner, Marcus Allen, fumbled, and defensive back Roger Jackson claimed the ball for the Lions. Two plays later, tailback Curt Warner, who rushed for 145 yards, scored from the 17. Only fifteen seconds had elapsed.

Penn State led only 14-7 in the second quarter when Allen put the ball on the turf again. That's when Wisniewski pulled off a big play that nevertheless must have drawn some guffaws from his teammates. When he bent down to pick the ball up, he kicked it — not just a gentle tap but a full-fledged boot-thumping that sent the ball skittering 18 yards down the sideline. Wisniewski finally managed to run the ball down and fall on it, setting up a field goal by Brian Franco. The Lions never looked back.

Remember that time you wrecked the car when you spilled hot coffee on your lap? That cold morning you fell out of the boat? The time you gave your honey a tool box for her birthday?

Formal education notwithstanding, we all make some dumb moves sometime because time spent in a classroom is not an accurate gauge of common sense. Folks impressed with their own smarts often grace us with erudite pronouncements that we intuitively recognize as flawed, unworkable, or simply wrong.

A good example is the observation that great intelligence and scholarship are not compatible with faith in God. That is, the more we know, the less we believe. But any incompatibility occurs only because we begin to trust in our own wisdom rather than the wisdom of God. We forget, as Solomon did, that God is the ultimate source of all our knowledge and wisdom and that even our ability to learn is a gift from God.

Not smart at all.

*I don't hire anybody not brighter than I am. If they're not smarter than me, I don't need them.*

— Bear Bryant

**Being truly smart means trusting in God's wisdom rather than only in our own knowledge.**

# WEATHERPROOFED

**Read Nahum 1:3-9.**

*"His way is in the whirlwind and the storm, and clouds are the dust of his feet" (v. 3b).*

**C**ool and dry" was the weather forecast for game day. Penn State's coaches relied on that forecast, and as a result, they almost didn't make it to their own stadium.

Head coach Rip Engle expected that forecast to be accurate when he ignored a light snowfall and herded his players into buses for the customary 20-mile ride to their retreat on the eve of the game against Fordham on Nov. 7, 1953. Around midnight, assistant coaches Jim O'Hora and Joe Paterno became concerned because the snowfall was not letting up.

In the morning, the snow was so heavy that the team bus couldn't navigate the back roads to the camp and thus couldn't get to the team. O'Hora and Paterno jogged about a mile through the snow to locate the missing bus. They didn't find it.

Engle decided on a plan of attack. He armed two cooks with rifles and told them to fire shots if the bus showed up. He then sent eleven players ahead to clear a path, and the rest of the players filed out to form a search party of their own. "This bedraggled group trundled through the drifts" until they heard the crack of a rifle from the cooks. The bus had been sighted!

Bone-weary, the players boarded the bus and, after a tedious, harrowing ride on the icy highways, arrived shortly before the scheduled kickoff time. In contrast the Fordham team had started out early, encountered no difficulty on the highway, and arrived shortly after noon for the 1:30 p.m. kickoff. Embarrassed, Engle had to plea with his Fordham counterpart to give his team an extra thirty minutes. The coach told Engle not to worry. "The delay won't lessen our desire to win," he said.

Despite their weather-related difficulties, the Lions won 28-21.

A thunderstorm washes away your golf game or the picnic with the kids. During that storm, lightning knocks out the electricity just as you settle in at the computer. A snowstorm forces you to cancel plans to visit the parents. A hurricane blows away your beach trip.

For all our technology and all our knowledge, we are still at the mercy of the weather, able only to get a little more advance warning than in the past. The weather answers only to God. Rain and hail will fall where they want to; snow will be totally inconsiderate of something as important as a Penn State football game.

We stand mute before the awesome power of the weather, but we should be even more awestruck at the power of the one who controls it, a power beyond our imagining. Neither, however, can we imagine the depths of God's love for us, a love that drove him to die on a cross for us.

*The only way I'd worry about the weather is if it snows on our side of the field and not theirs.*
*— Former baseball manager Tommy Lasorda*

**The power of the one who controls the weather**
**is beyond anything we can imagine,**
**but so is his love for us.**

# HUGS AND KISSES

**Read John 15:5-17.**

*"Now remain in my love" (v. 9b).*

One time while a Big Ten game was still going on, a Penn State player climbed into the stands and hugged her parents. In this case, it was perfectly all right.

After a 79-64 win over Illinois on Jan. 18, 2004, Penn State guard Kelly Mazzante nonchalantly sat at a table in the media room of the Bryce Jordan Center picking at a bandage on her right hand. She was "far from oblivious to what had just transpired but not all that concerned with it either." "I think our whole team knew it was going to happen and when it did, it happened, it was over," she said.

"It," though, was a really big deal, Mazzante's apparent indifference notwithstanding. With her 24 points in the win for the No. 8 Lady Lions, Mazzante had become the Big Ten conference's all-time leading scorer for women's basketball. She had needed nine points to claim the record and did it with two free throws with 7:05 left in the first half. The record Bryce Jordan Center crowd stood en masse and cheered. Penn State called time out to allow Mazzante's teammates to mob her and cameramen to get their photographs for history.

The Illinois head coach came over and shook Mazzante's hand. Then with the impetus of a little push from Penn State coach Rene Portland, Mazzante went into the stands to hug her parents, Louis and Julia. Julia was in tears long before her daughter made it into her arms, and Kelly admitted she had to struggle to avoid letting her own tears flow. Julia said of her daughter, "All she did was hug me and say, 'Don't cry mom, I love you.' And that said it all."

Four days later, Mazzante scored 29 points in a 75-56 win over Minnesota to become the Big Ten's all-time scorer, male or female. She finished her All-American career with 2,919 points. Amid some more hugs, her No. 13 jersey was retired on Dec. 29, 2004.

That friend from college you haven't seen for a while. Your family, including that aunt with the body odor. We hug them all, whether in greeting, in good-bye, or simply as a spontaneous display of affection. The act of physically clutching someone tightly to us symbolizes how closely we hold them in our hearts.

So whether you are a profligate hugger or a more judicious dispenser of your hugs, a hug is an act of intimacy. Given that, the ultimate hugger is almighty God, who, through Christ, continuously seeks to draw us closer to him in love. A good hug, though, takes two, so what God seeks from us is to hug him back.

We do that by keeping him close in our hearts, by witnessing for his Son through both words and deeds. To live our lives for Jesus is to engage in one long, refreshing heartwarming hug with God.

*I wasn't planning on it, but [coach] Rene [Portland] gave me a little nudge.*
— *Kelly Mazzante on hugging her parents*

**A daily walk with Christ means we are so close to God that we are engaged in one long, joyous hug with the divine.**

DAY 86

# ONE OF THOSE THINGS

**Read Isaiah 55:6-13.**

*"For my thoughts are not your thoughts, neither are your ways my ways" (v. 8).*

Aaron Harris pulled off one of the most memorable runs in Penn State football history. Only a week later, one of those things in life effectively ended both his college and football careers.

As a redshirt freshman fullback in 1996, Harris opened up lanes for Curtis Enis. The two of them lumbered for 1,797 yards and 26 touchdowns. This powerful ground game was the main reason *Sports Illustrated* picked the Lions No. 1 in the 1997 preseason.

Sure enough, Penn State started out 4-0 and then hosted Ohio State on Oct. 11 in what figured to be the biggest game of the season. The Buckeyes led 27-17 late in the third quarter, and the coaches called "36 slant," a favorite play because it usually caught defenses by surprise.

The ball went to Harris with Enis blocking. Harris bolted up the middle and "ended up getting Ping-Ponged around a little," but nobody brought him down. "Next thing I know there's [quarterback] Mike McQueary in front of me leading me down the field. Nobody else." Harris' 51-yard rumble ignited the crowd and the team. Penn State went on to win 31-27.

Seven days later, though, against Minnesota, Harris' season ended with a torn ACL. He played in 1998 with a bulky knee brace that slowed him down; he rushed for only 112 yards. In 1999, undiagnosed arthritis set in. By the end of the season, he could barely walk and had to have help getting dressed. When the team ran onto the field for the Alamo Bowl, Harris told a scout-team player, "Don't leave me. Don't make me look like that guy limping in the back who's dead weight to the team."

That's the way Harris' college career ended, and he went undrafted by the NFL. That injury was just one of those things.

You've probably had a few of "those things" in your own life: bad breaks that occur without regard to justice, morality, or fair play. You wonder if everything in life is random with events determined by a chance roll of some cosmic dice. Is there really somebody scripting all this with logic and purpose?

Yes, there is; God is the author of everything.

We know how it all began; we even know how it all will end. It's in God's book. The part we play in God's kingdom, though, is in the middle, and that part is still being revealed. The simple truth is that God's ways are different from ours. After all he's God and we are not. That's why we don't know what's coming our way, and why "those things" catch us by surprise and dismay us when they do occur.

What God asks of us is that we trust him. As the one — and the only one — in charge, he knows everything will be all right for those who follow Jesus.

*Sometimes the calls go your way, and sometimes they don't.*
*— Olympic gold medalist Dr. Dot Richardson*

**Life confounds us because, while we know the end and the beginning of God's great story, we are part of the middle, which God is still writing.**

# NOT WHAT THEY SEEM

### Read Habakkuk 1:2-11.

*"Why do you make me look at injustice? Why do you tolerate wrong? Destruction and violence are before me; there is strife, and conflict abounds" (v. 3).*

The Kansas players were already celebrating their Orange-Bowl win over Penn State. But hold on. Everything wasn't as it seemed.

The Nittany Lions and the Jayhawks got together in Miami on New Year's night 1969 and put on one of the most exciting Orange Bowls ever. The Lions of 1968 were 10-0; only Army, a 28-24 win, had played them close. Kansas was 9-1 and the Big Eight champions with an offense that averaged 38 points a game.

The Hawks seemed to have the game locked up with a 14-7 lead and the ball with only two minutes left to play, but the Penn State defense lived up to its reputation On successive plays, defensive tackle Mike Reid — a 1969 All-America — sacked the Kansas quarterback for thirteen yards worth of losses. The Jayhawks had to punt, and All-American safety Neal Smith partially blocked the kick. With 1:16 to play, Penn State had the ball at midfield.

In the Nittany Lions' huddle, halfback Bob Campbell told his quarterback, Chuck Burkhart, to forget about the short sideline pass. "Throw downfield for the left goalpost. I'll be there," he said. Burkhart did and Campbell was, hauling in the pass before being downed at the three. On third down, Burkhart bootlegged around his left end for the first rushing TD of his college career.

# NITTANY LIONS

Joe Paterno eschewed the tie. "If we couldn't win, we'd lose," he said after the game. The Lions appeared to lose when a pass was knocked away, and the Jayhawk celebration started. But a flag put a halt to the party; Kansas had twelve men on the field. Films later revealed they had had twelve men on the field for the entire goal-line series, even the State touchdown. This time, Campbell got around his left end for the two-point conversion, and things were exactly what they seemed. Penn State had a 15-14 win.

Just like football, in life sometimes in things aren't what they seem. In our violent and convulsive times, we must confront the possibility of a new reality: that we are helpless in the face of anarchy; that injustice, destruction, and violence are pandemic in and symptomatic of our modern age. It seems that anarchy is winning, that the system of standards, values, and institutions we have cherished is crumbling while we watch.

But we should not be deceived or disheartened. God is in fact the arch-enemy of chaos, the creator of order and goodness and the architect of all of history. God is in control. We often misinterpret history as the record of mankind's accomplishments — which it isn't — rather than the unfolding of God's plan — which it is. That plan has a clearly defined end: God will make everything right. In that day things will be what they seem.

*Unlike any other business in the United States, sports must preserve an illusion of perfect innocence.*
*— Author Lewis H. Lapham*

**The forces of good and decency often seem
helpless before evil's power, but don't be fooled:
God is in control and will set things right.**

# ATTITUDE CHECK

**Read 1 Thessalonians 5.**

*"Give thanks in all circumstances, for this is God's will for you in Christ Jesus" (v. 18).*

**A**ttitude instilled in her since her childhood had much to do with the success of the most honored women's volleyball player in Penn State history.

Megan Hodge "has been one of the best athletes of any sport ever to walk the University Park campus," said the *Centre Daily Times* shortly before Hodge closed out her stellar career by leading the Lions to the 2009 national championship, their third straight.

Hodge was so good that an opposing coach introduced herself to Hodge's parents and told them, "I'm very happy I'm never going to have to see your daughter in the collegiate ranks again." Hodge was the 2009 National Player of the Year and the Big Ten Player of the Year for the second time. She was a four-time All-America, only the fifth player in the history of women's college volleyball to be so honored. The outside hitter finished her career as only the second Penn State player in history to have more than 2,000 kills. *ESPN* named her its Academic All-American of the Year.

Hodge had both the natural athleticism and the height to be a star. That height — 6'4" of it — also had a lot to do with the attitude that contributed to her success. When she walks into a room, she does so with "an extra air of confidence" that should not, however, "be mistaken for any kind of strut." That walk was the result of something her parents constantly reminded her to do.

"She's tall," her mother said, declaring the obvious. "One thing we told her when she was very young, 'Don't ever curl your back.'" In other words, Hodge was to acknowledge her height. "Stand straight," her parents told her. "Square your shoulders."

With a confident attitude born of her parents' advice, Megan Hodge squared her shoulders and stood tall — especially when she played volleyball at Penn State.

How's your attitude? You can fuss because your house is not as big as some, because a coworker talks too much, or because you have to take pills every day. Or you can appreciate your home for providing warmth and shelter, the co-worker for the lively conversation, and the medicine for keeping you reasonably healthy.

Whether life is endured or enjoyed depends largely on your attitude. An attitude of thankfulness to God offers you the best chance to get the most out of your life because living in gratitude means you choose joy in your life no matter what your circumstances. This world does not exist to satisfy you, so chances are it will not.

True contentment and joy are found in a deep, abiding relationship with God. The appropriate way to approach that relationship is not with haughtiness or anger but with respect and gratitude for all God has given you.

*An awesome attitude is best described as a 'bad case of the wants.'*
*— Former Georgia assistant, Ga. Southern head coach Erk Russell*

**Your attitude goes a long way
toward determining the quality of your life
and your relationship with God.**

# A GOOD NEIGHBOR

**Read Luke 10:30-37.**

*"'Which of these three do you think was a neighbor to the man who fell into the hands of robbers?'" The expert in the law replied, 'The one who had mercy on him.' Jesus told him, 'Go and do likewise'" (vv. 36, 37).*

Once upon a time, before stringent NCAA regulations, a coach could actually help his boys out when they needed it.

One such coach was Dick Harlow, who played tackle at Penn State in 1910 and '11. After graduation, he stayed on as assistant coach before being named head coach in 1915. He was 20-8 from 1915-17 before leaving for the military. Harlow "pioneered modern defensive schemes," including "coordinated stunts to get around or between blockers rather than trying to overpower them." He was inducted into the College Football Hall of Fame in 1954.

Harlow the coach was tough, driving his players mercilessly at practice. A player hobbled back to his quarters one day and told his roommate they had had live blocking at practice. "We dumped each other all over the field," he said. "Great heavens," his friend exclaimed. "And what will you be doing tomorrow?" "Tomorrow," the player replied, "we start in with the hand grenades."

Harlow the man was a different story, however. After he retired in 1947, he reviewed his records and discovered that over the years he had loaned a considerable amount of money to his players for "books, illness, trouble at home or even to go home for the holiday." The total was about $27,000, a pretty good sum even for those days when the dollar had a different value.

That he could do that was evidence of a different era. So was the fact that with impeccable integrity athletes paid back their loans in those days. Only one loan of $165 was outstanding, and Harlow knew exactly why it was never repaid: "The boy was killed in World War II."

Ask most of us who our neighbor is and we'll probably start rattling off the names of the folks who live nearby; they live in our "neighborhood." We swap Christmas presents and support each other when illness or death strikes. We drive their kids to school sometimes, grill out together, and gather to watch the Nittany Lions on TV. Neighbors are our friends, a product of proximity and common interests and temperaments.

Jesus, however, redefined what it means to be a good neighbor. It has nothing to do with geography or a shared fanaticism for the Lions. Instead, it has everything do with the heart. Helping others out as Dick Harlow did isn't just a nice thing to do. It's actually a way of life for Christians, a direct, clear-cut commandment from Jesus himself. We are to be neighbors by helping our neighbors, the ones — wherever they live, whoever they are — who need mercy, love, and kindness from us.

We love God perfectly by loving our neighbors purely.

*If you burn your neighbor's house down, it doesn't make your house look any better.*
— *Lou Holtz*

**We are good neighbors to others
because God first was a good neighbor to us.**

# BLIND JUSTICE

### Read Micah 6:6-8.

*"He has showed you, O man, what is good. And what does the Lord require of you? To act justly and to love mercy and to walk humbly with your God" (v. 8).*

Let's just get the truth right out in the open: The Nittany Lions were robbed of the 1994 football championship.

Poll voters apparently were determined not to allow the Lions to win the title no matter what they did. Case in point: On Oct. 29, the top-ranked Lions beat Ohio State 63-14. Ohio State! And they fell to No. 2 behind Nebraska. "We *dropped!*" exclaimed PSU linebacker Willie Smith, "railing at the madness." "Sixty-three to 14, and we dropped! What do they want us to do to these teams?"

It wasn't fair, but there was nothing Penn State could do that they didn't do on the field. They went 11-0 and crushed Oregon State 38-20 in the Rose Bowl. All that "didn't really matter, because no victory would have been convincing enough. Nebraska swept the polls. Penn State finished second."

Obviously frustrated, Joe Paterno finally couldn't resist some politicking. He pointed out how Kansas State and Oklahoma, "two teams that were supposedly tougher than anybody we played," both lost their bowl games. All-American receiver Bobby Engram was also unconvinced of Nebraska's prowess. "Nebraska barely beat Iowa State [28-12]. *Iowa State*," he said. "Nebraska had trouble with Oklahoma [13-3]. I watched Oklahoma [in a 31-6 loss

# NITTANY LIONS

to BYU in the Copper Bowl]. Man, Oklahoma [stinks]."

The Nittany Lions had no doubts who was the best team in the country. When All-American quarterback Kerry Collins presented Paterno with the game ball from the Rose Bowl, he said, "This is for the greatest bowl coach in history. And the coach of the national champions."

If only justice had been done.

Where's the justice when cars fly past you just as a state trooper pulls you over? When a con man swindles an elderly neighbor? When crooked politicians treat your tax dollars as their personal slush fund? When children starve?

Injustice enrages us, but anger by itself is not enough. The establishment of justice in this world has to start with each one of us. The Lord requires it of us. For most of us, a just world is one in which everybody gets what he or she deserves.

But that is not God's way. God expects us to be just and merciful in all our dealings without consideration as to whether the other person "deserves" it. The justice we dispense should truly be blind.

If that doesn't sound "fair," then pause and consider that when we stand before God, the last thing we want is what we deserve. We want mercy, not justice.

*Deep inside, I guess we all knew that the national championship had already been decided [before the Rose Bowl].*
*— Penn State cornerback Brian Miller*

**God requires that we dispense justice and mercy**
**without regards to deserts, exactly what we pray**
**we will in turn receive from God.**

# BEING DIFFERENT

### Read Daniel 3.

*"We want you to know, O king, that we will not serve your gods or worship the image of gold you have set up"* (v. 18).

**W**hen he was at Penn State, John Urschel was different.

It wasn't that he was a third-team All-American guard and a two-time first-team All-Big Ten honoree who was taken in the fifth round of the 2014 NFL draft that made him different. After all, greatness on the gridiron certainly isn't rare at Penn State.

No, what made Urschel different was that he was great in football and in math. *Really* great at that math. When he finished up at Penn State in the spring of 2014, he had three degrees. He earned an undergraduate degree in mathematics in three years, a master's in math his fourth year, and a second master's in math education during his fifth or redshirt senior year. He was right consistent the whole time, too; in each degree he finished with a 4.0 grade-point average.

Urschel also taught Math 041 — Trigonometry and Analytic Geometry — to undergrads. Head football coach Bill O'Brien used a color-coded chart to keep track of which players would come to practice late or leave early for class. Green, blue, red, and yellow represented freshman, sophomore, etc. And then a purple showed up. "I've never seen that before," O'Brien said. So he asked his "academic guy" what was up with the purple. "That's

# NITTANY LIONS

Urschel," he was told. "He's not taking a class. He's teaching one."

Urschel's mother wanted him to go to MIT. "I wanted bigger football," he said. "We settled on Princeton." But when Penn State came calling his senior year, he fell in love with the campus.

"I love my university, and I love my team," said this personification of the student-athlete. He loved them about as much as he loves his math.

While we live in a secular society that constantly pressures us to conform to its principles and values, we serve a risen Christ who calls us to be different. Therein lies the great conflict of the Christian life in contemporary America.

But how many of us really consider that even in our secular society we struggle to conform? We are all geeks in a sense, even though we may not be as proficient at math as John Urschel is. We can never truly conform because we were not created by God to live in such a sin-filled world in the first place. Thus, when Christ calls us to be different by following and espousing Christian beliefs, principles, and practices, he is summoning us to the lifestyle we were born for.

The most important step in being different for Jesus is realizing and admitting what we really are: We are children of God; we are Christians. Only secondarily are we citizens of a secular world. That world both scorns and disdains us for being different; Jesus both praises and loves us for it.

*His chalk talks are in another galaxy.*
— *Head coach Bill O'Brien on John Urschel*

**The lifestyle Jesus calls us to is different from that of the world, but it is the way we were born to live.**

DAY 92

# OLD-FASHIONED

### Read Leviticus 18:1-5.

*"You must obey my laws and be careful to follow my decrees. I am the Lord your God" (v. 4).*

**N**ot too pretty!" shouted State center A.Q. Shipley. "Win's a win, baby," retorted receiver Deon Butler. Both Lions were dead-on as they left the field after an exhibition of old-fashioned football.

The 8-0 Nittany Lions met 7-1 Ohio State in Columbus on Oct. 25, 2008, in what was basically a showdown for the Big Ten title. Pundits expected one of the high-scoring shootouts common in contemporary college football. Instead, they got an old-fashioned defensive slugfest one writer called "paleolithic." He was left wondering "how far these teams set offensive football back over the course of three hours."

Penn State won 13-6 in a game dominated and controlled by a pair of stout, swarming defenses. The game ultimately turned on two big plays pulled off by — of course — the Lion defense.

With a 6-3 lead and 11 minutes left to play, Ohio State faced a third-and-one at midfield. The Buckeyes called for a quarterback sneak. Penn State defensive coordinator Tom Bradley anticipated the play and dialed up a linebacker blitz. The OSU signal caller read it and took the run outside. He was met by senior safety Mark Rubin, who punched the ball loose. Linebacker Navorro Bowman recovered it for the Lions at the Buckeye 38. Seven plays later, backup quarterback Pat Devlin scored on a one-yard sneak.

Then with a half minute to play, the Penn State defense made one fitting, final play when senior cornerback Lydell Sargeant hauled in an interception in the end zone that clinched the win.

Neither offense did much in this exhibition of clean, hard-hitting, old-fashioned football that featured a wealth of off-tackle plays. As A.Q. Shipley so aptly described it, the game wasn't too pretty. And as Deon Butler so correctly said, a win was a win, even an old-fashioned one.

Usually, when we refer to some person, some idea, or some institution as old-fashioned, we deliver a full-fledged or at least a thinly veiled insult. They're out of step with the times and the mores, hopelessly out of date, totally irrelevant, and quite useless.

For the people of God, however, "old-fashioned" is exactly the lifestyle we should pursue. The throwbacks are the ones who value honor, dignity, sacrifice, and steadfastness, who can be counted on to tell the truth and to do what they say. Old-fashioned folks shape their lives according to eternal values and truths, the ones handed down by almighty God.

These ancient laws and decrees are still relevant to contemporary life because they direct us to a lifestyle of holiness and righteousness that serves us well every single day. Such a way of living allows us to escape the ultimately hopeless life to which so many have doomed themselves in the name of being modern.

*What we saw in Columbus was an exhibition of cave drawings.*
*— Writer Austin Murphy on the 2008 Penn State-OSU game*

**The ancient lifestyle God still calls us to
leads us to a life of contentment, peace, and joy,
which never grows old-fashioned.**

# FIREPROOF

### Read Malachi 3:1-5.

*"Who can endure the day of his coming? Who can stand when he appears? For he will be like a refiner's fire or a launderer's soap. He will sit as a refiner and purifier of silver" (vv. 2, 3a).*

To his horror and dismay, as he headed for a game, Penn State's head football coach spotted several of his players gallantly fighting a farmhouse fire along the highway.

Bob Higgins coached the Lions from 1930-48, winning 123 games. He was well known for drawing up exotic plays, even declaring he could do it in his sleep. He did just that one time, dreaming of a pass play two days before the 1942 game against Colgate. The play worked perfectly in his dream, so he used it. The result was a touchdown and a 13-10 win for the Nittany Lions.

During World War II, Higgins struggled to find enough able bodies to field a team. He resorted to a reliance upon players too young to serve in the military, especially freshmen. Young and rambunctious, they often drove their coach to distraction. During a trip to Syracuse, they bought all the chocolate bars the hotel had, tried to talk their way into a jitterbug contest, and risked injury by "racing full-tilt through the hotel's revolving doors."

None of that, however, matched what those freshman pulled on the way to the game. As Higgins rode along, he saw a farmhouse fire with a group battling to put it out. With a second look, he realized that his freshmen players were among the firefighters.

As one Nittany Lion described it, "Not content to stay on the ground, they were dangling from the roof of a nearby barn, their hands occupied with buckets, and their heads completely barren of everything, including the game on the next day."

The vast majority of us never face the horror and agony of a literal fire, even one we help to put out as Bob Higgins' freshmen did. For most of us, fire conjures up images of romantic evenings before a fireplace, fond memories of hot dogs, marshmallows, and ghost stories around a campfire, or rib eyes sizzling on a grill. Fire is an absolutely necessary tool.

Yet we appreciate that fire also has the capacity to destroy. The Bible reflects fire's dual nature, using it to describe almighty God himself and as a metaphor for both punishment and purification. God appeared to Moses in a burning bush and led the wandering Israelites by night as a pillar of fire. Malachi describes Jesus as a purifying and refining fire. Fire is also the ultimate symbol for the destructive force of God's wrath, a side to God we quite understandably prefer not to dwell upon. Our sin and disobedience, though, do not only break God's heart but also anger him.

Thus, fire in the Bible is basically a symbol for God's holiness. Whether that holiness destroys us or purifies us is the choice we make in our response to Jesus. We are, all of us, tested by fire.

*I hope once the war is over that someone will someday erect a monument to freshmen football coaches.*

— *Bob Higgins*

**God's holy fire is either the total destroyer or the ultimate purifier; we are fireproof only in Jesus.**

# ONE TOUGH COOKIE

### Read 2 Corinthians 11:21b-29.

*"Besides everything else, I face daily the pressure of my concern for all the churches" (v. 28).*

**M**att Millen's solution to the problem was simple: Lock his calcified arm in a vise and put weight on it until the calcium broke.

Millen was an All-American defensive tackle for Penn State in 1978 who went on to a 12-year NFL career that included four Super Bowl wins.

His decision to sign with the Nittany Lions resulted in some attempted sabotage by a sister. The Buffaloes of Colorado were recruiting him heavily, so Penn State assistant John Chuckran made a personal visit to Millen's home to sign him. They couldn't find the letter of intent Chuckran had mailed him, so the coach had another letter flown in and Millen signed up. Afterwards, he learned one of his younger sisters had hidden the letter. She wanted her brother to play for Colorado because she was a John Denver fan and she especially liked "Rocky Mountain High."

About those calcium deposits. When he was a junior in high school, Millen suffered an arm injury that resulted in calcification of the elbow so extensive that his arm was locked at a 45-degree angle. Doctors told him his football career was over.

Millen would have none of it; his first idea was hot water. That didn't work. So he figured maybe brute force would do it. He conned a teammate into joining him in the high school wood shop. There, Millen locked his elbow in a vise and had his buddy put all his weight on his forearm. Despite what must have been excruciating pain, the calcium refused to break up.

Next, Millen opted for sheer willpower. He went to the weight room, loaded up a bar, and began doing forearm curls. Willpower eventually won out; the calcium wasn't as tough as Millen was and eventually gave in. Millen went on with his football career.

You don't have to be a legendary Penn State defensive tackle to be tough. In America today, toughness isn't restricted to physical accomplishments and brute strength. Going to work every morning even when you feel bad, sticking by your rules for your children in a society that ridicules parental authority, making hard decisions about your aging parents' care often over their objections — you've got to be tough every single day just to live honorably, decently, and justly.

Living faithfully requires toughness, too, though in America chances are you won't be imprisoned, stoned, or flogged this week for your faith as Paul was. Still, contemporary society exerts subtle, psychological, daily pressures on you to turn your back on your faith and your values. Popular culture promotes promiscuity, atheism, and gutter language; your children's schools have kicked God out; the corporate culture advocates amorality before the shrine of the almighty dollar.

You have to hang tough to keep the faith.

*Winning isn't imperative, but getting tougher in the fourth quarter is.*
— *Bear Bryant*

**Life demands more than mere physical toughness;
you must be spiritually tough too.**

# NOTES
### (by Devotion Day Number)

1     "the nature of the game . . . an intercollegiate football game.": Ken Rappoport, *Tales from Penn State Football* (Champaign, IL: Sports Publishing, L.L.C., 2007), p. 3.

1     Among the school's 170 students . . . activity" for the students.: Ken Rappoport, *The Nittany Lions: Penn State Football* (Tomball, TX: The Strode Publishers, Inc., 1987), p. 22.

1     the faculty had no opposition . . . best players for the team.: Rappoport, *The Nittany Lions*, p. 23.

1     only twelve uniforms were available.: Rappoport, *Tales from Penn State Football*, p. 3.

1     he had the only ball.: Rappoport, *Tales from Penn State Football*, p. 3.

1     A later game against Dickinson College was cancelled.: Rappoport, *The Nittany Lions*, p. 23.

1     We can use some football here.: Rappoport, *The Nittany Lions*, p. 22.

2     People across the country . . . just a lot of wind.": Rick Reilly, "Guts, Brains and Glory," *Sports Illustrated*, 12 Jan. 1987, http://sportsillusrated.cnn.com/vault/article/magazine/MAG1126846/index.htm, April 30, 2010.

2     "We played for the national championship on Sept. 27: Reilly.

2     One Miami flanker bragged about . . . You've chosen your own death row.": Reilly.

2     "The weather was cool. The ball was slippery,": Reilly.

2     They kept talking about how little our defensive backs were, but they'd never been hit by them.: Reilly.

3     "a scene straight out of High Noon." . . . five consecutive times.: Richard O'Brien, "Who Were Those Masked Men?" *Sports Illustrated*, April 9, 1990, http://sportsillustrated.cnn.com/vault/article/magazine/MAG1137015/index.htm, April 30, 2010.

4     "the big Ten confrontation of the year.": Tim Layden, "All on the Line," *That Perfect Season* (New York City: Time, Inc., 1995), p. 38.

4     Collins saw a Michigan. . . going with the ball.": Tim Layden, "The Lions Roar to the Fore," *Sports Illustrated*, Oct. 24, 1994, http://sportsillustrated.cnn.com/vault/article/magazine/MAG1005826/index.htm, April 30, 2010.

5     "In the second half, we . . . work really well for us.": Jeff Rice, "New Kids on the Clock," *Restoring the Pride* (Champaign, IL: Sports Publishing L.L.C., 2005), p. 38.

5     We needed this kind of [comeback] win to boost our team.: Rice, p. 39.

6     When she was in the third . . . a player named Clint Seace,: Kelly Whiteside, "Happy Days," *Sports Illustrated*, Feb. 7, 1994, http://sportsillustrated.cnn.com/vault/article/magazine/MAG1148156/index.htm, April 30, 2010.

6     a tradition that had begun . . . arch of a high-heeled shoe. "They hurt,": Whiteside.

7     "a powerful charger . . . his last game against Pitt.: Rappoport, *Tales from Penn State Football*, p. 14.

7     In his official capacity . . . and all her baby chicks.": Rappoport, *Tales from Penn State Football*, p. 14.

7     He went into virtual . . . the gloves hindered his work.: Rappoport, *Tales from Penn State Football*, p. 16.

8     Nineteen inches of snow . . . the seats, and the walkways.: Jordan Hyman, *Game of My Life Penn State* (Champaign, IL: Sports Publishing, L.LC., 2006), p. 173.

8   "Those things were stinging,": Hyman, p. 172.

8   offense coordinator Franny Ganter . . . right side on field goals,:Hyman, p. 171.

8   "We just pulled a guard and kicked the guy out, "Nastasi recalled. "It was pretty easy.": Hyman, p. 172.

8   "It was perfect,": Hyman, p. 172.

8   "I just took the snap, picked it up and ran.": Hyman, p. 173.

8   I thought we were going . . . they converted the fake field goal.: Hyman, p. 174.

9   "the dirty girl"? . . . think about things like that.": Gordon Brunskill, "Celebration Continues for Nittany Lions," *Centre Daily Times*, Feb. 12, 2008.

9   I was pretty disgusting. . . . my entire life.: Brunskill, "Celebration Continues."

10  "the best football player I ever coached.": "John Cappelletti," *Wikipedia, the free encyclopedia*, http://en.wikipedia.org/wiki/John_Cappelletti, May 4, 2010.

10  In a New York ballroom . . . and his tears began.: Rappoport, *Tales from Penn State Football*, p. 72.

10  "They say I've shown courage . . . an inspiration to me.": Rappoport, *Tales from Penn State Football*, p. 72.

10  Amidst thunderous applause and sobs, . . . table to hug Joey.: John Sanchez, "John Cappelletti's Special Gift to His Dying Brother," *associatedcontent.com*, Dec. 5, 2006, http://www.associatedcontent.com/article/93855, May 4, 2010.

10  Before the '73 West Virgina . . . scored his fourth touchdown.: Rappoport, *Tales from Penn State Football*, p. 71.

10  Johnny just gave you his Heisman Trophy.: Sanchez.

11  With a few belongings, a letter . . . Wally Triplett left home in 1945: Hyman, pp. 2-3.

11  Early in the 1940s, Dave Alston. . . a tonsillectomy and never lettered.: Hyman, p. 4.

11  that included veterans who had . . . "We play together, we stay together.": Hyman, p. 6.

11  None of the hotels in Dallas . . . eighteen miles outside of town.: Rappoport, *The Nittany Lions*, p. 181.

11  This is life. Let's live it and not be afraid.: Hyman, p. 11.

12  in a community in which . . . to basketball and softball.: Jordan Hyman and Ken Rappoport, *Playing for JoePa* (Champaign, IL: Sports Publishing L.L.C., 2007), p. 103.

12  Harris "never wasted time dreaming . . . in our whole life.": Hyman and Rappoport, p. 104.

12  "She would tell the younger . . . It was funny.": Hyman and Rappaport, p. 108.

13  Harry Groves didn't know . . . there was no clock involved.": Cecily Cairns, "Groves Leaves Remarkable Marks on and off PSU Track," *Centre Daily Times*, May 21, 2006.

13  uninterested in doing anything else . . . "I just jumped at applying,": Cairns.

14  "State College is located in . . . played away from home.": Rappoport, *The Nittany Lions*, p. 99.

14  "It is impossible for [Penn State]. . . necessary to go someplace else.": Rappoport, *The Nittany Lions*, p. 99.

14  8,500 miles: Rappoport, *The Nittany Lions*, p. 99.

14  The Nittany Lions were starting to be called the 'Nittany Nomads.': Rappoport, *The Nittany Lions*, p. 99.

15  If the especially intense practices . . . time to play some football.'": Jeff Rice, "Nittany Lions Finally Trap Wolverines in Ann Arbor," *Centre Daily Times*, Oct. 25, 2009.

15  This victory is a little bit sweet for us,": Rice, "Nittany Lions Finally

Trap."

15  It got through to us how much . . . only to him but to Penn State.: Rice, "Nittany Lions Finally Trap."

16  Four days after the team's . . . can't feel sorry for ourselves.": Heather A. Dinich, "Six Is Enough," *Centre Daily Times*, Jan. 4, 2004.

16  "You like our rotation?": Dinich.

16  The Bisons rotated fourteen players . . . to try to tire the Lion players out.: Dinich.

17  he stepped off the plane . . . I travel incognito.": Rappoport, *The Nittany Lions*, pp. 232-33.

17  The airport restaurant refused . . . belonged in the game at all.: Rappoport, *The Nittany Lions*, p. 233.

18  "Son, this is gonna be a big week . . . and found a blue jersey.: Hyman, p. 149.

18  He had been behind two kickers . . . expected to be redshirted.: Hyman, p. 148.

18  "I was scared to death,": Hyman, p. 149.

18  "I'd never felt so sick in my life,": Hyman, p. 149.

18  "shuttling him into an off week . . . in the field goal column.": Hyman, p. 149.

18  "The roll, as it goes, was on.": Hyman, p. 149.

18  Confidence for an athlete is a. . . But you know when you have it.: Hyman, p. 150.

19  Harlow broke an ankle. . . . out there with a broken leg.": Rappoport, *Tales from Penn State Football*, p. 12.

20  In the summer, she noticed . . . I went completely numb.": Mark Myers, "Lucas' Struggles Shift Perspective," *The Daily Collegian*, April 27, 2005, http://www.collegian.psu.edu/archive/2005/04/04-27-05tdc/04-27-05dsports-05.asp, June 25, 2010.

20  her faith actually grew during. . . that I could have had [a heart attack].": Myers.

20  That fall she was pronounced . . . healthy as I've ever been.": Walt Moody, "Lucas Is Back Where She Knew She Would Be," *Centre Daily Times*, Feb. 23, 2005.

20  I don't look at my situation . . . and I can help people.': Moody, "Lucas Is Back."

21  the Nittany Lions held a team meeting . . . where they would go.: Rich Scarcella, *Stadium Stories* (Guilfod, CN: The Globe Pequot Press, 2004), p. 66.

21  Always wanting to play the . . . his team to go to the Cotton Bowl.: Scarcella, p. 66.

21  an "open revolt" . . . "a disappointing set of circumstances.": Scarcella, p. 67.

21  Several of the African-American . . . for a third straight year.: Scarcella, p. 66.

21  The team's vote eventually . . . by playing in the Cotton Bowl.: Scarcella, p. 67.

21  Paterno agreed to let the team be home for Christmas.: Scarcella, p. 67.

21  The Lions were widely viewed as having avoided the best possible team.: Scarcella, p. 67.

21  When Ohio State lost, we realized we had blown a chance at the national championship.: Scarcella, p. 67.

22  Higgins was a stickler . . . I wear size 14.": Rappoport, *Tales from Penn State Football*, p. 41.

22  he failed to show for . . . that bum in Thorpe's uniforms?": Rappoport, *Tales from Penn State Football*, pp. 40- 41.

23  Butler knew out of high school . . . I was always practicing hard,": Walt Moody, "Butler Works Way into Penn State's Record Book," *Centre Daily Times*, Nov. 16, 2008.

23  When Butler broke a tie with . . . "I'm glad we kept moving from there,": Moody.

23  "despicable, vile, unprincipled scoundrels.": John MacArthur, *Twelve Ordinary Men* (Nashville: W Publishing Group, 2002), p. 152.

23  When a kid like [ Deon Butler] comes in here as a walk-on and he turns out to be as good as he is, it's great.: Moody.

24   When she was a freshman . . . I can't do this,": Jeff Rice, "Heady Player," *Centre Daily Times*, Sept. 8, 2003.

24   Before her senior season, she said. . . shape because I want to win.": Rice, "Heady Player."

25   When Paterno was an assistant . . . "It took awhile.": "Sue Paterno More Than Coach's Wife at Penn State," *Sporting News*, Aug. 28, 2009, http://www.sportingnews.com/college-football/article/2009-08-28, June 15, 2010.

25   she tried to make every game, . . . five dollars between us.: Rappoport, *Tales from Penn State Football*, p. 84.

25   As soon as I heard . . . it was too late then.: Rappoport, *Tales from Penn State Football*, p. 84.

26   Paterno decided to go for the tie . . . about a foot apart.: Lou Prato, *Game Changers* (Chicago: Triumph Books, 2009), p. 32.

26   guard Eric Cunningham, fullback . . .and Guman scored untouched.: Prato, p. 33.

26   Only after the game did Fusina . . . had actually been two yards,: Prato, p. 32.

26   I lied a little.: Prato, p. 32.

27   "one of the two or three best . . . have fielded since 1986.": Ron Bracken, "Rivera a Man of Good Character," *Centre Daily Times*, May 1, 2005.

27   Shortly after he signed . . . refused to take the money back.: Bracken, "Rivera a Man of Good Character."

27   It wasn't right for me to keep the money.: Bracken, "Rivera a Man of Good Character."

28   "who occupies a prominent spot . . . fans around the world.": Prato, p. 2.

28   Joe Paterno sent out a play . . . four guys as receivers.: Ken Rappoport, *Penn State Nittany Lions: Where Have You Gone?* (Champaign, IL: Sports Publishing L.L.C., 2005), p. 140.

28   "We had all seams covered, . . . had not come to Garrity,: Rappoport, *Penn State Nittany Lions: Where Have You Gone?*, p. 141.

28   "I threw the ball as far as I could,": Prato, p. 4.

28   He jumped to his feet "with . . . "the biggest reception in Penn State history.": Prato, p. 5.

29   Jose Palacios has nearly died of . . . security agents who detained him at gunpoint.: RyanHockensmith, "Without Limits," *Centre Daily Times*, Feb. 11, 2001.

29   "If there's any time Palacios' . . . headphones on, and no helmet.": Hockensmith.

29   I love my bike. I'm . . . I don't wreck every day.: Hockensmith.

30   "but it was 125 pounds of talent.": Rappoport, *The Nittany Lions*," p. 85.

30   when he returned to campus in 1919, he was up to 145 pounds.": Rappoport, *The Nittany Lions*, p. 88.

30   "detested playing football . . . to practice every day.": Rappoport, *The Nittany Lions*, p. 85.

30   "We practiced every afternoon . . . for a little fellow.": Rappoport, *The Nittany Lions*, p. 88.

30   His family had little money, . . . wasn't with a scholarship.: Rappoport, *The Nittany Lions*, p. 86.

30   A Dartmouth player recalled . . . right out of the ballgame.": Rappoport, *The Nittany Lions*, p. 89.

30   "he would get worked up . . . like a small child.": Rappoport, *The Nittany Lions*, p. 85.

31   a "dreadful" 15-7 season-opening win over Maryland.: Scarcella, p. 6.

31   When the game ended, Paterno . . . mine just stunk worse than yours did.": Scarcella, p. 6.

31    "I thought we were great," Paaterno said. He also thought, "Boy, what a great coach I am.": Hyman, p. 61.

31    questioning his abilities.: Scarcella, p. 6.

31    On the bus ride home from Annapolis,: Hyman, p. 70.

31    a "dramatic" decision: Scarcella, p. 6.

32    Shipley got into his pre-sunrise . . . for a little extra motivation.: Jeff Rice, "Rise and Shine," *Centre Daily Times*, July 31, 2005.

32    It's what we live for, eh?: Rice, "Rise and Shine."

33    The squad was 7-0 when . . . their weight for the next match.: Andy Elder, "One and Only," *Centre Daily Times*, Jan. 31, 2003.

33    Wrestler Bob Homan recalled . . . to sweat and lose weight.": Elder, "One and Only."

33    Some will be grayer and heavier . . . what was and what could have been.: Elder, "One and Only."

34    Paterno was adamant about players' getting their degree.: Scarcella, p. 2.

34    He promised them that he would get their son an education.: Rappoport, *Tales from Penn State Football*, p. 66.

34    His last semester he finished . . . failed to graduate.: Rappoport, *Tales from Penn State Football*, p. 66.

34    Heller never thought much about . . . for him any more.": Rappoport, *Tales from Penn State Football*, p. 67.

35    The powers-that-be had . . . school of athletic scholarships.: Rappoport, *The Nittany Lions*, p. 150.

35    "We couldn't even buy a meal for players,": Rappoport, *The Nittany Lions*, p. 154.

35    That and the Depression . . . periods of its sports history.": Rappoport, *Tales from Penn State Football*, p. 37.

35    "We couldn't beat a good high school team!": Rappoport, *The Nittany Lions*, p. 154.

35    After a 47-0 blowout . . . pounded him mercilessly.: Rappoport, *The Nittany Lions*, p. 150.

35    After the game, the coach's . . . of the paper's editor.: Rappoport, *Tales from Penn State Football*, p. 37.

35    When you get licked as often . . . over being a tough guy.: Rappoport, *Tales from Penn State Football*, p. 37.

36    I was thinking, 'Block this kick.' It just so happened, I got it. Aw man, I got Joe No. 324.: Prato, p. 128.

37    "the program was a laughingstock" in the spring.: Don Stewart, "Underrated Nittany Lions Wanted to Prove," *Centre Daily Times*, March 19, 2001.

37    forward Gyasi Cline-Heard thought . . . with no big-name recruits on hand.: Stewart.

37    But in the preseason, the team's . . . Penn State men's basketball on the map.: Stewart.

37    "to its highest point ever.": Stewart.

37    I love it when people underestimate us.: Stewart.

38    On a snowy night in January . . . after his car came to a rest.: Ron Bracken, "Fighting Back," *Centre Daily Times*, Sept. 13, 2003.

38    Alan Zemaitis always wore a . . . forehead. It hides the scars.: Bracken, "Fighting Back."

39    "the greatest football play I've ever seen.": Prato, p. 130.

39    "thrilling and electrifying.": Prato, p. 130.

39    Paterno acted on a hunch: Prato, p. 133.

**194**

39    The ball sat on the right hash, . . . Menhardt shanked it wide left;: Prato, p. 133.

39    he studied "performance enhancement . . . football team in 1978.: Prato, p. 133.

39    skimmed off the inside right . . . the greatest wins for Penn State,": Prato, p. 133.

39    When I hit it, I knew it was in the area.": Prato, p. 133.

40    With only one second left,: Rappoport, *Tales from Penn State Football*, p. 31.

40    The final whistle blew . . . roaring down on him.: Rappoport, *Tales from Penn State Football*, p. 31.

40    he lateraled to fellow . . . some 15,000 persons dumbfounded.": Rappoport, *Tales from Penn State Football*, p. 32.

40    Varsity cheerleader Izzy Heicklen . . . he ever got it back.: Rappoport, *Tales from Penn State Football*, p. 32.

41    "We've been shooting for it . . . "We're here to play.": David Comer, "Penn State Softball," *Centre Daily Times*, May 18, 2000.

41    Last year our goal was . . .to get further than that.: Comer, "Penn State Softball."

42    The university had decided to . . . conferences in intercollegiate athletics.": Kip Richeal, *Welcome to the Big Ten* (Champaign, IL: Sagamore Publishing, 1994), p. 7.

42    In the early 1980s, Joe Paterno . . . Syracuse, Temple, and Rutgers.: Richeal, p. 6.

42    That proposal fell through . . . joined the Big East in basketball.: Richeal, pp. 6-7.

42    The decision to move into the Big Ten was based almost exclusively on what was best for football: Richeal, p. 4.

42    "We were having a hard time maintaining the kind of program we were accustomed to,": Richeal, p. 6.

42    I was surprised at how quickly things developed.: Richeal, p. 3.

43    It's amazing. It's absolutely amazing.": David Comer, "Nittany Lions Finish Unlikely March to Title," *Centre Daily Times*, May 29, 2000.

43    they'd mosey over to . . . come on the field and roll over.": Comer, "Nittany Lions Finish."

43    "Its' unbelievable," . . . two games from North Carolina.: Comer, "Nittany Lions Finish."

43    With three starters missing because of injuries and/or illness,: Comer, "Nittany Lions Finish."

43    I don't think anyone thought we could do this.: Comer, "Nittany Lions Finish."

44    Ohio State's head coach adopted . . . stomped in the face.: "A Lesson in Penn State-Ohio State History," *blackshoediaries.com*, Nov. 5, 2009, http://www.blackshoe diaries.com/2008/10/22/637430, May 4, 2010.

44    Ohio State's coach decided . . . left on the clock.: "A Lesson in Penn State-Ohio State History."

45    "The Miracle of Mount Nittany," Jack McCallum,l "O.K., Time to Fasten Those Seat Belts," *Sports Illustrated*, Oct. 4, 1982, http://sportsillustrated.cnn.com/vault/ article/magazine/MAG1125981/index.htm, April 30, 2010.

45    "We practice the two-minute . . . minute left, we had 65 yards to go.": McCallum.

45    Junior Kirk Bowman came  . . earned his nickname, "Stonehands.": McCallum.

45    All I kept thinking about was Philippians 4:13: 'I can do all things through the Lord.': McCallum.

46    "never expected to be a coach": Rappoport, *The Nittany Lions*, p. 193.

46    "from as far down as . . . the Pennsylvania coal mines.: Rappoport, *The Nittany Lions*, p. 192.

46    He never even saw . . . the only job he could get.: Rappoport, *The Nittany Lions*, p. 193.

46    his hire came with the . . . who had never coached.: Rappoport, *The*

Nittany Lions, p. 195.

46    he called the staff together . . . "Everything worked out so well.": Rappoport, *The Nittany Lions*, pp. 196-97.

46    I think God made it simple. Just accept Him and believe.: Bettinger, Jim & Julie S., *The Book of Bowden* (Nashville, TN: TowleHouse Publishing, 2001), p. 47.

47    "We had them on the ropes . . . especially when it's to 15.": Gordon Brunskill, "Penn State Eclipses Top-Ranked UC Irvine," *Centre Daily Times*, May 5, 2006.

47    That's when the lights . . . delivered a blistering ace.: Brunskill, "Penn State Eclipses."

48    It was a bad idea . . . Nope. No way.": Ron Bracken, "Profile: Levi Brown," *Restoring the Pride* (Champaign, IL: Sports Publishing L.L.C., 2005), p. 98.

48    and he was going to be one . . . telling me where I have to play?": Bracken, "Profile: Levi Brown," p. 98.

48    "from a field of dreams to a field of screams.": Bracken, "Profile: Levi Brown," p. 98.

48    "Right now I'd have to . . . but I like it.": Bracken, "Profile: Levi Brown," p. 99.

48    I believe in Joe and he believed in me.: Bracken, "Profile: Levi Brown," p. 98.

49    We're a year away from a national championship.": Douglas S. Looney, "It Was the Pits for Pitt," *Sports Illustrated*, Dec. 7, 1981, http://sportsillustrated.cnn.com/vault/article/magazine/MAG112504/index.htm.

49    "was the only first-rate opponent": Looney.

49    We have four players who could . . .seven who could start for Pittsburgh.: Looney.

50    "in an era when young players were given such positions." Rappoport, *The Nittany Lions*, p. 55.

50    The forward pass had been . . . and so they were hired,': Rappoport, *The Nittany Lions*, p. 55.

50    He had players who were older than he was,: Rappoport, *The Nittany Lions*, p. 56.

50    "In those days, pep talks . . . inspire a football team.": Rappoport, *The Nittany Lions*, p. 56.

50    he regularly wrote to . . . all the answers he could.: Rappoport, *The Nittany Lions*, p. 55.

50    the youngest head football coach in the country.: Rappoport, *Tales from Penn State Football*, p. 10.

51    "A bitter, bitter loss to take": Jennifer Wheaton James, "Penn State Hoops Memories: Season Marked Trip to the Top," *Centre Daily Times*, Feb. 9, 2008.

51    a scheduling conflict at Rec Hall . . . too well with the Seminole fans.: James.

51    Playing on an injured ankle she had sprained in warm-ups,: James.

51    Jan. 3 lived up to everything we had hoped for in that locker room ten months earlier.: James.

52    "Nixon's gesture . . . caused a furor in Pennsylvania.": Scarcella, p. 65.

52    by offering Joe Paterno and . . . trophy and shove it," and hung up.: Scarcella, pp. 67, 69.

52    "deprived some kids of the opportunity to be called national champions.": Scarcella, p. 69.

52    I'd like to know how could . . . much about college football in 1969?: Scarcella, p. 7.

53    "I don't think we quite realized how good they were offensively,": Jeff Rice, "Roar in the Fourth," *Centre Daily Times*, Nov. 1, 2009.

53    the Penn State players knew . . . and get into those guys.": Rice, "Roar in the Fourth."

53    That whole first half, . . . started putting points up.: Rice, "Roar in the Fourth."

54    Conceding that the task . . . in the 1948 Cotton Bowl.: Scott Brown and Michael

Weinreb, "10 to Remember," *The Daily Collegian*, Oct. 16, 1993, http://www.collegian.psu.edu/archive/1993.10/10-16-93cm, June 14. 2010.

55 "enough league championships to fill all of her fingers with rings,": David Comer, "Lady Lions Have Come a Long Way Lately," *Centre Daily Times*, March 28, 2000.

55 "Coach told us that . . . And here we are,": Comer, "Lady Lions Have Come a Long Way Lately."

55 With exactly one minute left . . . I think I ruined her outfit.": David Comer, "Penn State Advances to Its First Final Four," *Centre Daily Times*, March 28, 2000.

55 This is incredibly sweet.: Comer, "Lady Lions Have Come a Long Way."

56 "He threw some passes . . . a college quarterback throw,": Rappoport, *The Nittany Lions*, p. 334.

56 "He had to become more . . . hour after hour every day.: Rappoport, *The Nittany Lions*, p. 334.

56 He received more than his share . . . to work too hard.": Rappoport, *Tales from Penn State Football*, p. 78.

56 My buddy and that projector . . . to go back to school.: Rappoport, *The Nittany Lions*, p. 334.

57 the Blue Band began in 1899 with . . . was hired in 1914.: "Traditions & History," *Penn State Blue Band*, http://blueband.psu.ed/history/, July 15, 2010.

57 In 1913, sophomore Jimmy Leyden . . . and the entire student body.: Prato, p. 71.

57 The first blue uniforms appeared . . . in New York City in 2005.: "Traditions & History."

58 We're too old for this. It's almost past my bedtime.": Jeff Rice, "Freshman Kelly Kicks Nittany Lions to Triple-Overtime Win after Midnight," *Centre Daily Times*, Jan. 4, 2006.

58 [Two] coaches that don't want their . . . seemed as though it would never end.: Jeff Rice, "Freshman Kelly Kicks Nittany Lions to Triple-Overtime Win."

59 When the Big Ten jumpers . . . the lives of other athletes.": Ron Bracken, "For Nittany Lions' Audu, Blessed Is the Giver," *Centre Daily Times*, June 13, 1999.

59 the possibility of amputation loomed large: Bracken, "For Nittany Lions' Audu."

59 Turner eventually needed eight surgeries: "Track and Field: Jumper to Try It One More Time," *The New York Times*, May 2, 2000, http://wwww.nytimes.com/2005/05/02/sports/track-and-field-jumper, June 28, 2010.

59 will wear a brace . . . rest of his life.: Bracken, "For Nittany Lions' Audu."

59 News of Turner's injury . . . but it got out.: Bracken, "For Nittany Lions' Audu."

59 That plaque would have been nice . . . to give back to people.: Bracken, "For Nittany Lions' Audu."

60 had a tooth knocked out . . . handed him his tooth.: Rappoport, *The Nittany Lions*, p. 109.

60 the Bisons were without . . . careful of your bad ankle.": Rappoport, *The Nittany Lions*, pp. 134-35.

60 Each time Diehl carried the call . . . made to American football.": Rappoport, *The Nittany Lions*, p. 135.

61 Billy Sullivan, owner of the then-woeful . . . repeatedly came out ahead.: Rappoport, *Tales from Penn State Football*, p. 74.

61 "Money, Cape Cod, security . . . behind all the time.": Rappoport, *Tales from Penn State Football*, pp. 74-75.

61 So he accepted Sullivan's offer. . . . flattered by the dough.": Rappoport, *Tales from Penn State Football*, p. 75.

61 You went to bed with a millionaire and woke up a pauper.:

Rappoport, *Tales from Penn State Football*, p. 75.

62    Red Carlson turned into . . . cookies to the Panther players.: Mickey Bergstein, "Penn State Hoops Memories: Fans Witnessed a Circus of a Basketball Game in '52," *Centre Daily Times*, March 9, 2008.

63    Frank Spaziani played all four . . . at quarterback in '67.: Ron Bracken, "Spaziani a Diamond for Perfect Season," *Centre Daily Times*, Sept. 6, 2003.

63    In the spring of his senior year . . . his nickname, "Diamond Spaz.": Bracken, "Spaziani a Diamond."

63    "Don't get the idea . . . because I'm Italian.": "Frank Spaziani," *Wikipedia, the free encyclopedia*, http://en.wikipedia.org/wiki/Frank_Spaziani, June 26, 2010.

63    *ESPN's* Chris Spielman has referred . . . lab coats in Diamond Spaz's honor: "Frank Spaziani."

63    "It's a business, it's a job,": Bracken, "Spaziani a Diamond."

63    "But I'd rather be playing someone else,": Bracken, "Spaziani a Diamond."

64    "In every unbeaten season, . . . everything hangs in the balance,": Ron Bracken, "Nittany Lions Shake off Irish," *Centre Daily Times*, Nov. 17, 2007.

65    Butville wrestled in high school and . . . 3.5 GPA in mechanical engineering.: Andy Elder, "Lights, Camera . . . Butville!" *Centre Daily Times*, Jan. 18, 1997.

65    On Jan. 3, 1997, starting 150-pounder . . . "I didn't want to give up.": Elder, "Lights, Camera."

65    Who would have thought he . . . with that bad ankle?: Elder, "Lights, Camera."

66    "I thought I was a pretty good tight . . . to know what he was talking about.: Ron Bracken, "He's a Lineman Now," *Centre Daily Times*, Sept. 11, 2004.

66    When they moved me to tackle, . . . specials are during the week.": Bracken, "He's a Lineman Now."

66    I like to say I'm a slim tackle. I don't look like a 370-pounder.: Bracken, "He's a Lineman Now."

67    "We ran three tackles," . . . would play two positions.": Rappaport, *Penn State Nittany Lions: Where Have You Gone?"*, p. 95.

67    "have his arm around me, . . . few other players could know.: Rappaport, *Penn State Nittany Lions: Where Have You Gone?*, p. 95.

67    "And he said, 'They're gonna . . . 'He's crazy.'": Rappaport, *Penn State Nittany Lions: Where Have You Gone?*, p. 95.

67    "He was saying, 'They're gonna . . . 'The guy's lost it.'": Rappaport, *Penn State Nittany Lions: Where Have You Gone?*, p. 95.

68    Joe Paterno gave a pre-game . . . swayed to "Auld Lang Syne.": Dwight Kier, "Paterno's Pregame Pep Talk Inspires Lady Lions," *Centre Daily Times*, Jan. 6, 1996.

68    Coach Rene Portland tried to stick to her pre-game routine: Dwight Kier, "Saying Goodbye to Rec Hall," *Centre Daily Times*, Jan. 6, 1996.

68    Paterno asked her if . . . full access to the facility.: Kier, "Paterno's Pregame Pep Talk."

68    no one envisioned women . . . to play in the Jordan Center.": Kier, "Saying Good-Bye to Rec Hall."

68    It's time to move on.: Kier, "Saying Goodbye to Rec Hall."

69    The player who was . . . Engle's all-time favorite: Rappaport, *The Nittany Lions*, p. 223.

69    He was nicknamed "Riverboat Richie" . . . dangerous at all times,": Rappaport, *The Nittany Lions*, p. 223.

69    "He looked like a . . . when he played football.": Rappaport, *The Nittany Lions*, p. 225.

69    Instead of punting on fourth . . . had expressly ordered a punt.: Rappoport, *The Nittany Lions*, p. 225.

69    Lucas, though, had realized . . . heavy rush to advantage.: Rappoport, *The Nittany Lions*, pp. 223, 225.

69    Engle was never quite sure . . . "I treat it as a suggestion.": Rappoport, *The Nittany Lions*, p. 225.

70    All day in short yardage . . . grabbed him from behind.: Craig Neff, "They're Lion Low No More," *Sports Illustrated*, 17 Oct. 1983, http://sportsillustrated.cnn.com/vault/article/magazine/MAG1121388/index.htm, April 30, 2010.

70    I could sense it coming.: Neff.

71    Assistant coach Dick Harlow . . . never throw another one.: Rappoport, *Tales from Penn State Football*, p. 24.

71    nobody told head coach . . . going on around here.": Rappoport, *Tales from Penn State Football*, pp. 24-25.

71    the trick play "took the heart" . . . first two minutes of play.": "On This Day in Penn State History: November 27, 1919," *blackshoediaries.com*, Nov. 28, 2008, http://www.blackshoediaries.com.section/penn-state-history, May 4, 2010.

71    Anyone could have done . . . to catch the pass.": Dan Jenkins, Marvin Hyman, Gary Ronberg, "Not a Passing Fancy," *Sports Illustrated*, Sept. 20, 1965, http://sportsillustrated.cnn.com/vault/article/magazine/MAG1077673/index.htm.

72    He had simply worn out . . . He had lost 20 pounds.: Kimberly Jones, "Gaudio Eager to Get Career Going Again," *Centre Daily Times*, Oct. 15, 1995.

72    "It's not that bad," he . . . made it look worse than it was.": Kimberly Jones, "Slated for Surgery, Gaudio Plays Hard," *Centre Daily Times*, Dec. 3, 1995.

72    With the minutes I played, it'll swell tonight.: Jones, "Slated for Surgery."

73    Senior quarterback Daryll Clark wanted . . . a wobbly, incomplete pass.": Jeff Rice, "Clark Delivers in Final Game," *Centre Daily Times*, Jan. 2, 2010.

73    We ran into a couple of pit  . . . it done when we needed to.: Rice, "Clark Delivers."

74    He found himself stuck as a . . . you averaged seven yards a carry,": Hyman, p. 79.

74    Paterno turned to the man . . . great football coach someday.': Hyman, p. 80.

74    No more calls home.: Hyman, p. 80.

75    "No swimmer at Penn State ever had a better start to a career.": Justin Kunkel, "Swimmer Finding Her Smile Again," *The Daily Collegian*, March 17, 2004, http://www.collegian.psu.edu/archive/2004/03/3-17-04tdc/03-17-04dsports-07.asp, June 24, 2010.

75    "I was barely sleeping. I had constant . . . was worth all the time and stress.": Kunkel.

75    During her sophomore season, . . . get nervous before meets.: Jeff Rice, "Nittany Lion Swimmer Happy to Be Back in the Pool," *Centre Daily Times*, Feb. 11, 2005.

75    In October of 2002, she walked into . . . granted reinstatement to the team.: Kunkel.

75    My heart told me and my head told me that I needed a break.: Rice, "Nittany Lion Swimmer."

76    Ryland didn't know whom he might be . . . Penn State would be on television.": Ron Bracken, "Love of the Game," *Centre Daily Times*, Sept. 6, 2003.

76    When he started against . . . to my younger brothers and sisters.": Bracken, "Love of the Game."

76    Your grandfather is smiling down on you.: Bracken, "Love of the Game."

77    "as good a linebacker as  we've had here.": Rappoport, *The Nittany Lions*, p. 316.

77    Paterno had Buttle ticketed . . . "You're a pretty smart guy,": Rappoport, *The Nittany Lions*, p. 317.

77    The fired-up Lions held . . . his helmet against a locker.: Rappoport, *Tales from Penn State Football*, p. 88.

77    It bounced off and hit . . . moving in slow motion.: Rappoport, *Tales from Penn State Football*, p. 90.

77    Can't we even get through the team prayer without an injury?: Rappoport, *Tales from Penn State Football*, p. 90.

78    "Just when Penn State basketball had . . . consider to be the basketball gallows.": Richeal, p. 70.

78    "to put a wrap on the biggest upset in school history.": Richeal, p. 72.

78    Bobby Knight admitted to State's coach, Bruce Parkhill, that the Lions deserved to win.: Richeal, p. 74.

78    On the night when David almost . . . en officials had looked for.: Richeal, p. 76.

79    "Oregon never has played . . . both frozen and bored.: Rappoport, *The Nittany Lions*, p. 229.

79    The city provided snowplows . . . over the heads of the players.: Rappoport, *Tales from Penn State Football*, p. 54.

79    "Instead, the players turned medium . . . one big mud hole.: Rappoport, *Tales from Penn State Football*, p. 55.

80    most pundits said the most . . . four or five losses.: Ron Bracken, "Editor's Note," *Restoring the Pride* (Champaign, IL: Sports Publishing L.L.C., 2005), p. 4.

80    It was classic Joe Paterno: . . . just enough points to win.: Ron Bracken, "This Game Lines Up with Other Great Wins," *Restoring the Pride* (Champaign IL: Sports Publishing L.L.C., 2005), p. 65.

80    He was sprung free by a block from right tackle Andrew Richardson.: Jeff Rice, "Penn State Upsets No. 6 Ohio State," *Restoring the Pride* (Champaign, IL: Sports Publishing L.L.C., 2005), p. 57.

80    "back in the territory their predecessors took for granted": Bracken, "This Game Lines Up with Other Great Wins," p. 62.

80    This was a chance . . . on the national stage.: Bracken, "This Game Lines Up with Other Great Wins," p. 65.

81    was attending Penn State . . . to give up soccer for tennis,": Gordon Brunskill, "Glory Years," *Centre Daily Times*, Sept. 16, 2005.

81    Who are you?: Brunskill, "Glory Years."

82    "swashbuckling, tight-fitting . . . they wore "snug beanies."": Rappoport, *The Nittany Lions*, p. 26.

82    "wanted something bright and attractive,": Rappoport, *The Nittany Lions*, p. 26.

82    one of the three students appointed to choose two colors: Cyndi Burk, "Pink & Black?" *The Daily Collegian*, Sept. 24, 1988, http://www.collegian.psu.edu/archive/1988/09/04-24-88cm/09-24-88cm-01.asp, May 4, 2010.

82    red and orange were out of . . . accepted the gaudy combination.: Rappoport, *The Nittany Lions*, p. 26.

82    Both the school's football team . . . became the new fashion trend of the 80s.": Burk.

82    After a few weeks of exposure . . . to plain old black and white.: Rappoport, *The Nittany Lions*, p. 26.

82    in March 1890, the student boy . . . Penn State team to don the new duds.: Burk.

82    I think I'd feel pretty silly wearing pink and black.: Burk.

83    I felt like an idiot.": N. Brooks Clark, "Fiesta Bowl," *Sports Illustrated*, Jan. 11, 1982, http://sportsillustrated.cnn.com/vault/article/magazine/MAG1125137/index.htm.

83    The Trojans accused them of intentionally . . . their stories by the light of matches.":
      Clark.

83    "We mangled them. We intimidated them. We shocked them.": Clark.

83    sent the ball skittering 18 yards down the sideline.: Clark.

84    Cool and dry" was the weather forecast for game day.: Rappoport, *The Nittany
      Lions*, p. 207.

84    when he ignored a light snowfall . . . was not letting up.: Rappoport, *The Nittany
      Lions*, p. 207.

84    In the morning, the snow . . . They didn't find it.: Rappoport, *The Nittany Lions*,
      p. 208.

84    He armed two cooks . . . before the scheduled kickoff time.: Rappoport, *The Nittany
      Lions*, p. 209.

84    the Fordham team had started. . . arrived shortly after noon: Rappoport, *The Nittany
      Lions*, p. 208.

84    Engle had to plea with . . . lessen our desire to win,": Rappoport, *The Nittany Lions*,
      p. 209.

85    After a 79-64 win over Illinois . . . it happened, it was over,": Jeff Rice, "As Usual,
      Mazzante Basks Briefly in Her Own Glory," *Centre Daily Times*, Jan. 19, 2004.

85    with two free throws with 7:05 . . . 'Don't cry, mom, I love you.' And that said it
      all.": Rice, "As Usual."

85    I wasn't planning on it, but [coach] Rene [Portland] gave me a little nudge.: Rice,
      "As Usual."

86    This powerful ground game was the . . . Lions No. 1 in the 1997 preseason.: Hyman,
      p. 180.

86    The coaches called "36 slant," a . . . down the field. Nobody else.": Hyman, p. 181.

86    He played in 1998 with a . . . back who's dead weight to the team.": Hyman, p. 183.

87    In the Nittany Lions' huddle, . . . I'll be there,": Rappoport, *Tales from Penn State
      Football*, p. 69.

87    "If we couldn't win, we'd lose,": Rappoport, *Tales from Penn State Football*, p. 69.

87    Films later revealed . . . even the State touchdown.: Rappoport, *Tales from Penn State
      Football*, p. 71.

88    "has been one of the . . . the University Park campus,": Gordon Brunskill, "Leaving
      Her Mark," *Centre Daily Times*, Dec. 4, 2009.

88    an opposing coach introduced . . . the collegiate ranks again.": Brunskill, "Leaving
      Her Mark."

88    When she walks into . . . "Square your shoulders.": Brunskill, "Leaving Her Mark."

89    "pioneered modern defensive . . . trying to overpower them.": "Dick Harlow,"
      *Wikipedia, the free encyclopedia*, http://en.wikipedia.org/wiki/Dick_Harlow,
      May 4, 2010.

89    A player hobbled back . . . with the hand grenades.": Rappoport, *Tales from Penn
      State Football*, pp. 11-12.

89    After he retired in 1947, . . . was about $27,000,: Rappoport, *Tales from Penn State
      Football*, p. 19.

89    Only one loan of $165 . . . killed in World War II.": Rappoport, *Tales from Penn State
      Football*, p. 19.

90    "We dropped!" . . . to do to these teams?": Tim Layden, "Roses with Thorns," *That
      Perfect Season* (New York City: Time Inc., 1995), p. 76.

90    All that "didn't really matter, . . . Penn State Finished second.: Layden,
      "Roses with Thorns," p. 79.

90    He pointed out how . . . Man, Oklahoma [stinks].": Layden, "Roses
      with Thorns," p. 79.

90   "This is for the greatest . . . coach of the national champions.": Layden, "Roses with Thorns," p. 85.

90   Deep inside, I guess . . . had already been decided.: Layden, "Roses with Thorns," p. 79.

91   Head football coach Bill O'Brien used . . . and I love my team,": Erik Brady, "Penn State's John Urschel Has Love for Math and Football," *USA Today*, July 24, 2013, http://www.usatoday.com/story/sports/ncaaf/bigten/2013/07/24/john-urschel-penn-state-nittany-lions-math-education-2581867.

91   His chalk talks are in another galaxy.: Brady, "Penn State's John Urschel."

92   Not too pretty!" shouted State center A.Q. Shipley. "Win's a win, baby," retorted receiver Deon Butler.: Austin Murphy, "We Are Defense," *Sports Illustrated*, Nov. 3, 2008, http://sportsillustrated.cnn.com/vault/article/magazine/MAG1147460/index.htm.

92   one writer called "paleolithic." . . . the course of three hours." Murphy, "We Are Defense."

92   Penn State defensive coordinator Tom . . . took the run outside.: Murphy, "We Are Defense."

92   What we saw in Columbus was an exhibition of cave drawings.: Murphy, "We Are Defense."

93   He was well known for . . . result was a touchdown: Rappaport, *Tales from Penn State Football*, p. 43.

93   During a trip to Syracuse, . . . the hotel's revolving doors.": Rappaport, *Tales from Penn State Football*, p. 44.

93   As Higgins rode along, . . .the game on the next day.": Rappaport, *Tales from Penn State Football*, pp. 43-44.

93   I hope once the war . . . to freshmen football coaches.: Rappaport, *Tales from Penn State Football*, p. 44.

94   Colorado was recruiting him . . . began doing forearm curls.: Ron Bracken, "Former PSU, NFL Linebacker Walked to Beat of His Own Drum," *Centre Daily Times*, Jan. 14, 2001.

# WORKS CITED

Bergstein, Mickey. "Penn State Hoops Memories: Fans Witnessed a Circus of a Basketball Game in '52." *Centre Daily Times*. 9 March 2008.

Bettinger, Jim & Julie S. *The Book of Bowden*. Nashville: TowleHouse Publishing, 2001.

Bracken, Ron. "Editor's Note." *Restoring the Pride: Penn State's 2005 Championship Season*. Champaign, IL: Sports Publishing L.L.C., 2005. 4.

-----. "Fighting Back: Zemaitis Recovers from Car Accident to Start for Nittany Lions." *Centre Daily Times*. 13 Sept. 2003.

-----. "For Nittany Lions' Audu, Blessed Is the Giver." *Centre Daily Times*. 13 June 1999.

-----. "Former PSU, NFL Linebacker Walked to Beat of His Own Drum." *Centre Daily Times*. 14 Jan. 2001.

-----. "He's a Lineman Now." *Centre Daily Times*. 11 Sept. 2004.

-----. "Love of the Game: Ryland Making the Most of His Opportunity." *Centre Daily Times*. 6 Sept. 2003.

-----. "Nittany Lions Shake Off Irish." *Centre Daily Times*. 17 Nov. 2007.

-----. "Profile: Levi Brown." *Restoring the Pride: Penn State's 2005 Championship Season*." Champaign, IL: Sports Publishing L.L.C., 2005. 98-99.

-----. "Rivera a Man of Good Character." *Centre Daily Times*. 1 May 2005.

-----. "Spaziani a Diamond for Perfect Season." *Centre Daily Times*. 6 Sept. 2003.

-----. "This Game Lines Up with Other Great Wins." *Restoring the Pride: Penn State's 2005 Championship Season*. Champaign, IL: Sports Publishing L.L.C., 2005. 62-65.

Brady, Erik. "Penn State's John Urschel Has Love for Math and Football." *USA Today*. 24 July 2013. http://www.usatoday.com/story/sports/ncaaf/bigten/2013/07/24/john-urschel-penn-state-nittany-lionis-math-education-2581867/.

Brown, Scott and Michael Weinreb. "10 to Remember: Looking Back after 999 Penn State Football Games." *The Daily Collegian*. 16 Oct. 1993. http://www.collegian.psu.edu/archive/1993/1010-16-93cm.

Brunskill, Gordon. "Celebration Continues for Nittany Lions." *Centre Daily Times*. 12 Feb. 2008.

-----. "Glory Years: Penn State to Honor 1954 and '55 National Champs." *Centre Daily Times*. 16 Sept. 2005.

-----. "Leaving Her Mark." *Centre Daily Times*. 4 Dec. 2009.

-----. "Penn State Eclipses Top-Ranked UC Irvine." *Centre Daily Times*. 5 May 2006.

Burk, Cyndi. "Pink & Black?" *The Daily Collegian*. 24 Sept. 1988. http://www.collegian.psu.edu/archive/1988/09/09-24-88cm/09-24-88cm-01.asp.

Cairns, Cecily. "Groves Leaves Remarkable Marks on and off PSU Track." *Centre Daily Times*. 21 May 2006.

Clark, N. Brooks. "Fiesta Bowl." *Sports illustrated*. 11 Jan. 1982. http://sportsillustrated.cnn.com/vault/article/magazine/MAG1125137/index.htm.

Comer, David. "Lady Lions Have Come a Long Way Lately." *Centre Daily Times*. 28 March 2000.

-----. "Nittany Lions Finish Unlikely March to Title." *Centre Daily Times*. 29 May 2000.

-----. "Penn State Advances to Its First Final Four." *Centre Daily Times*. 28 March 2000.

-----. "Penn State Softball." *Centre Daily Times*. 18 May 2000.

"Dick Harlow." *Wikipedia, the free encyclopedia*. http://en.wikipedia.org/wiki/Dick_Harlow.

Dinich, Heather A. "Six is Enough: Short-Handed Nittany Lions Hold off Bucknell." *Centre Daily Times*. 4 Jan. 2004.

Elder, Andy. "Lights, Camera . . . Butville!" *Centre Daily Times*. 18 Jan. 1997.

-----. "One and Only: Penn State's Lone National Championship Team to Be Honored." *Centre Daily Times*. 31 Jan. 2003.

"Frank Spaziani." *Wikipedia, the free encyclopedia*. http://en.wikipedia.org/wiki/Frank_ Spaziani.

Hockensmith, Ryan. "Without Limits." *Centre Daily Times*. 11 Feb. 2001.

Hyman, Jordan. *Game of My Life Penn State: Memorable Stories of Nittany Lions Football*. Champaign, IL: Sports Publishing L.L.C., 2006.

Hyman, Jordan and Ken Rappaport. *Playing for JoePa: Inside Joe Paterno's Extended Football Family*. Champaign, IL: Sports Publishing L.L.C., 2007.

James, Jennifer Wheaton. "Penn State Hoops Memories: Season Marked Trip to the Top." *Centre Daily Times*. 9 Feb. 2008.

Jenkins, Dan, Marvin Hyman, and Gary Ronberg. "Not a Passing Fancy." *Sports Illustrated*. 20 Sept. 1965. http://sportsillustrated.cnn.com/vault/article/magazine/ MAG1077673/index.htm.

"John Cappelletti." *Wikipedia, the free encyclopedia*. http://en.wikipedia.org/wiki/John_ Cappelletti.

Jones, Kimberly. "Gaudio Eager to Get Career Going Again." *Centre Daily Times*. 15 Oct. 1995.

-----. "Slated for Surgery, Gaudio Plays Hard." *Centre Daily Times*. 3 Dec. 1995.

Kier, Dwight. "Paterno's Pregame Pep Talk Inspires Lady Lions." *Centre Daily Times*. 6 Jan. 1996.

-----. "Saying Goodbye to Rec Hall." *Centre Daily Times*. 6 Jan. 1996.

Kunkel, Justin. "Swimmer Finding Her Smile Again." *The Daily Collegian*. 17 March 2004. http://www.collegian.psu.edu/archieve/2004/03/03-17-04tdc/03-17- 04dsports-07.asp.

Layden, Tim. "All on the Line." *That Perfect Season: Penn State 1994*. New York City: Time Inc., 1995, 38-45.

-----. "The Lions Roar to the Fore." *Sports Illustrated*. 24 Oct. 1994. http://sportsillustrated. cnn.com/vault/article/magazine/MAG1005826/index.htm.

-----. "Roses with Thorns," *That Perfect Season: Penn State 1994*. New York City: Time Inc., 1995, 72-85.

"A Lesson in Penn State-Ohio State History." *blackshoediaries.com*. 5 Nov. 2009. http:// www.blackshoediaries.com/2008/10/22/637430.

Looney, Douglas S. "It Was the Pits for Pitt." *Sports Illustrated*. 7 Dec. 1981. http://sports illustrated.cnn.com/vault/article/magazine/MAG1125044/index.htm.

MacArthur, John. *Twelve Ordinary Men*. Nashville: W Publishing Group, 2002.

McCallum, Jack. "O.K., Time to Fasten Those Seat Belts." *Sports Illustrated*. 4 Oct. 1982. http://sportsillustrated.cnn.com/vault/article/magazine/MAG1125981/index.htm.

Moody, Walt. "Butler Works Way into Penn State's Record Book." *Centre Daily Times*. 16 Nov. 2008.

-----. Lucas Is Back Where She Knew She Would Be." *Centre Daily Times*. 23 Feb. 2005.

Murphy, Austin. "We Are Defense." *Sports Illustrated*. 3 Nov. 2008. http://sports illustrated.cnn.com/vault/article/magazine/MAG1147460/index.htm.

Myers, Mark. "Lucas' Struggles Shift Pespective." *The Daily Collegian*. 27 April 2005. http://www.collegian.psu.edu/archive/2005/04/04-27-05tdc/04-27-05dsports-05. asp.

Neff, Craig. "They're Lion Low No More." *Sports Illustrated*. 17 Oct. 1983. http:// sportsillustrated.cnn.com/vault/article/magazine/MAG1121388/index.htm.

O'Brien, Richard. "Who Were Those Masked Men?" *Sports Illustrated*. 9 April 1990. http://sportsillustrated.cnn.com/vault/article/magazine/MAG1137015/index.htm.

"On This Day in Penn State History: November 27, 1919." *blackshoediaries.com*. 28 Nov.

2008. http://www.blackshoediaries.com/section/penn-state-history.

Prato, Lou. *Game Changers: The Greatest Plays in Penn State Football History*. Chicago: Triumph Books, 2009.

Rappoport, Ken. *Penn State Nittany Lions: Where Have You Gone?* Champaign, IL: Sports Publishing L.L.C., 2005.

-----. *Tales from Penn State Football*. Champaign, IL: Sports Publishing, L.L.C., 2007.

-----. *The Nittany Lions; Penn State Football*. Tomball, TX: The Strode Publishers, Inc., 1987.

Reilly, Rick. "Guts, Brains and Glory." *Sports Illustrated*. 12 Jan. 1987. http://sports illustrated.cnn.com/vault/article/magazine/MAG126846/index.htm.

Rice, Jeff. "As Usual, Mazzante Basks Briefly in Her Own Glory." *Centre Daily Times*. 19 Jan. 2004.

-----. "Clark Delivers in Final Game." *Centre Daily Times*. 2 Jan. 2010.

-----. "Freshman Kelly Kicks Nittany Lions to Triple-Overtime Win after Midnight." *Centre Daily Times*. 4 Jan. 2006.

-----. "Heady Player: Psych Major Zinkavich Protects the Penn State Net." *Centre Daily Times*. 8 Sept. 2003.

-----. "New Kids on the Clock." *Restoring the Pride: Penn State's 2005 Championship Season*. Champaign, IL: Sports Publishing L.L.C., 2005. 34-39.

-----. "Nittany Lion Swimmer Happy to Be Back in the Pool." *Centre Daily Times*, 11 Feb. 2005.

-----. "Nittany Lions Finally Trap Wolverines in Ann Arbor." *Centre Daily Times*. 25 Oct. 2009.

-----. "Penn State Upsets No. 6 Ohio State." *Restoring the Pride: Penn State's 2005 Championship Season*. Champaign, IL: Sports Publishing L.L.C., 2005. 54-59.

-----. "Rise and Shine: A Tireless Worker, Shipley Aiming to Make Impact This Fall." *Centre Daily Times*. 31 July 2005.

-----. "Roar in the Fourth: Clark, Lions Stay Patient to Put Away Wildcats." *Centre Daily Times*. 1 Nov. 2009.

Richeal, Kip. *Welcome to the Big Ten: Penn State's Inaugural Football Season*. Champaign, IL: Sagamore Publishing, 1994.

Sanchez, John. "John Cappelletti's Special Gift to His Dying Brother." *associatedcontent.com*. 5 Dec. 2006. http://www.associatedcontent.com/article/93855.

Scarcella, Rich. *Stadium Stories: Penn State Nittany Lions*. Guilford, CN: The Globe Pequot Press, 2004.

Stewart, Don. "Underrated Nittany Lions Wanted to Prove." *Centre Daily Times*. 19 March 2001.

"Sue Paterno More Than Coach's Wife at Penn State." *Sporting News*. 28 Aug. 2009. http://www.sportingnews.com/college-football/article/2009-08-28.

"Track and Field: Jumper to Try It One More Time." *The New York Times*. 2 May 2000. http://www.nytimes.com/2000/05/02/sports/track-and-field-jumper.

"Traditions & History." *Penn State Blue Band*. http://blueband.psu.edu/history.

Whiteside, Kelly. "Happy Days." *Sports Illustrated*. 7 Feb. 1994. http://sportsillustrated.cnn.com/vault/article/magazine/MAG1148156/index.htm.

# NAME INDEX
## (LAST NAME, DEVOTION DAY NUMBER)

**206**

# SCRIPTURES INDEX
## (by DEVOTION DAY NUMBER)

# NITTANY LIONS